HIGHLY
SENSITIVE

BOOKS BY CAROL A. BROWN

The Mystery of Spiritual Sensitivity

AVAILABLE FROM DESTINY IMAGE PUBLISHERS

HIGHLY
SENSITIVE

CAROL A. BROWN

DESTINY IMAGE® PUBLISHERS, INC.

P.O. Box 310, Shippensburg, PA 17257-0310

"Speaking to the Purposes of God for This Generation and for the Generations to Come."

This book and all other Destiny Image, Revival Press, MercyPlace, Fresh Bread, Destiny Image Fiction, and Treasure House books are available at Christian bookstores and distributors worldwide.

For a U.S. bookstore nearest you, call 1-800-722-6774.
For more information on foreign distributors, call 717-532-3040.
Reach us on the Internet: www.destinyimage.com.

Trade Paper ISBN 13: 978-0-7684-3260-2
Hardcover ISBN 13: 978-0-7684-3464-4
Large Print ISBN 13: 978-0-7684-3465-1
Ebook ISBN 13: 978-0-7684-9107-4

For Worldwide Distribution, Printed in the U.S.A.
1 2 3 4 5 6 7 8 9 10 11 / 13 12 11 10

Dedication

Dedicated to the uncounted numbers of God's "Special Forces."
God made no mistake when He made you.

Acknowledgments

A DEBT OF THANKS TO MARK Sandford for his gracious assistance and theological editing. Thanks to my husband, David, for his unwavering belief in me and this project. Thanks to the many readers who kept asking when the next book was coming out! But most of all, my undying gratitude goes to Father God for calling me and walking with me every step of the way—even when I carried on like a camel during the difficult times!

Endorsements

Training in reproducible ministry skills for healing, maturity, and releasing unexpected new life—Carol has a unique and wonderful understanding of the gift of spiritual sensitivity. I used her first book as the focus of my women's journaling group, and they are looking forward to *Highly Sensitive: Understanding Your Gift of Spiritual Sensitivity!* I will be encouraging my patients to read it. This is groundbreaking work that Carol is doing, and if we want to understand and cooperate with the way that God created us, we would do well to allow Carol to teach us more and more about the gift of spiritual sensitivity.

Susan M. Austin MD, PLLC
Albany, New York

So many books on Christians and their identities read like a Whack-A-Mole game. Reflexively they whack anything that moves without thinking, using their theory of identity like a mallet to whack anyone who sticks his or her head up. There is very little thought that some people should not be whacked! With Carol's gentle approach, you will want to keep your head up, look around, and enjoy becoming alive. You will want to let your children and family come out of their holes as well.

Dr. E. James Wilder
Director, Shepherd's House

Highly Sensitive: Understanding Your Gift of Spiritual Sensitivity fills the gap! Our prayer-ministry students, their hearts heavy with compassion, need these practical teachings and exercises to learn to channel their compassion in ways that effectively help the person in need. I am so grateful for how Carol's work has helped me and for how this book will free others to minister more joyfully, freely, and effectively as well.

Lori N. Wright
Healing Hearts (Community of Grace)
Hayward, California

Burden Bearing: (verb)

To know or understand something of another person's inner state of being in some sensory way, carry the pain or trouble to the cross, and pray passionately, inviting Jesus into the situation or circumstance based upon what you have sensed from the person and from God's own heart. The Holy Spirit within you gathers up the burden from every place in you that it has gone, draws it through you, lifts it up and out of you, and places it on the cross of Christ. Natural burden bearers are highly sensitive. See the list of some of the symptoms of high sensitivity.

Symptoms of High Sensitivity/ Characteristics of a Burden Bearer

Do you:

- Have difficulty with bright lights, loud noises and large crowds (overstimulation)

- Need "recovery" time away from stimulation, noise, or activity

- Sometimes ask pointed questions that others consider inappropriate (They thought they had hidden their trouble better than that)

- Have a vivid imagination

- Stay attuned to family needs and try to "help," actively or passively, in whatever way you can

- Stay attuned to and are affected by others' moods

- Have times of excessive emotion—responses seem extreme, whether it be grief, anger, sadness, or tears over physical hurts

- Have times of uncharacteristic behavior when you don't "act like yourself"

- Have tender feelings that are easily hurt

- Appear shy and quiet

- Feel vulnerable to sadness or depression

- Feel you lose your individuality around strong personalities or intense inner turmoil and trouble

- See things others cannot see

- Know or sense things ahead of time

- Cut the tags out of your shirts and sweaters because they irritate

You may be coping with a highly sensitive nervous system, which is core to burden bearing and sensing the heart of God! It is a good thing!

Contents

Foreword

A**LL CHRISTIANS ARE COMMANDED TO** bear others' burdens (see Gal. 6:2). But some of us bear them even when not commanded to—and much of the time, we can't help it! From birth, God has graced some of us with an especially merciful and spiritually sensitive temperament. But if we don't call our sensitivity to death on the cross of Christ and let Him resurrect it in *His* strength, our penchant for carrying the world on our shoulders can drag us under. Carol helps you chuck the extra baggage.

My son Jasha is such a one as this. From the time he was a toddler he always "knew" when others were hurting—and oh, if he could only heal them all! I recall a time when his mom cried silently in the kitchen. Six-year-old Jasha couldn't possibly hear her from behind his upstairs bedroom door; but in his spirit he sensed her pain, and he scampered down to offer a hug and a promise that everything would be all right. Maureen and I could envision a 30-year-old Jasha still eager to take on loads far too heavy for him, rushing out to bandage the entire world, and facing spiritual burnout. In an effort to spare him of that, we assured him that although we appreciated his loving heart, he did not have to take care of Mom. His head understood, but getting his heart to grasp it was another thing.

Parents can't hide their children from every tussle in the daily school of hard knocks. But there were some influences from which we could hide him. Knowing that demons can project messages, we prayed to hide Jasha's spiritual ears. But he kept sensing others' pain even when out of the room, for God and demons are not the only sources of spiritual messages—there is one's own personal spirit as well.

Ezekiel scolded, *"Woe to the foolish prophets who follow their own spirit"* (Ezek. 13:3 NIV). Though Jasha's spiritual radio picked up a lot of random signals, he was otherwise unlike the prophets Ezekiel upbraided. They deliberately cast aside discretion and peered into a spiritual realm that God declares off-limits to anything but His gifts. They deserved Ezekiel's sharp rebuke. But what do you do with an innocent little guy like Jasha? What he did was accidental.

To a lesser degree this happens to most of us. Have you ever seen someone's car in their driveway and the lights and television were on, yet somehow you "knew" they weren't home? You went through the motion of knocking on the door, suspecting no one would answer—and you were right! Have you ever "known" that the phone was about to ring—and it did? You were not acting as a false prophet or a psychic. You didn't try to do these things. You committed no deliberate sins. They just happened.

Likewise, there are sensitive Christians who accidentally sense other's sorrows, angers, and fears, but mistakenly assume that these are their own feelings. Since they do not identify the true source of these feelings, they cannot know that they can release them to the cross through intercessory prayer. They get so loaded down with other people's pain that they become desperate to do something—

anything—to alleviate the feeling of powerlessness.

Like the false prophets of Ezekiel's day, some today choose to make deliberate use of their spiritual sensitivity. To their own peril, they embrace New Age "gifts," which attract demons. Others choose to follow Christ and embrace His gifts instead. But, not knowing how to dispose of or even identify the burdens their spirit is accruing, they groan under a burgeoning load, throw up their hands, and despairingly question what Jesus could possibly have meant when He said, "My burden is light." Other Christians just shut off their feelings in order to survive and end up hearing nothing from God at all. But that doesn't work either. Numbness doesn't keep the burdens from attaching. And it hurts even worse when the Novocain wears off.

How could we help Jasha avoid all of these fates? Thankfully, we had at our disposal the simple tools Carol presents in this book (some of which she has borrowed from us). She outlines the proper use of God's gifts, and how to tell what is and is not God's voice. She teaches you to impose healthy boundaries on your compulsive urge to single-handedly rescue the world. She speaks of learning to trust God—even though He allowed the world to get so messy! She shows you how to find true identity *in Christ,* not in the gifts that enable you to bear burdens. Most blessedly, she discusses childhood issues that cause others' burdens to get "stuck" in you instead of passing through you to the cross.

We recently helped teenage Jasha work through one of these issues. After spending his short lifetime standing strong for every broken heart around him, he at last found someone attuned to his own weary heart. But this threatened to expose a similar need in his friend who promptly fled the pain, leaving Jasha to tend to his, alone. Those are rough waters for any teenage boy, but Jasha felt as if he had gone over the falls. He couldn't sleep (he hadn't slept well for years anyway—he was too worried about everyone he loved). He couldn't study. At times he couldn't stop crying.

If we didn't already possess the tools Carol outlines in these pages, we might have disparaged what appeared to be an "overreaction," and tried to talk some "sense" into him. But that would have tempted him to shut down his heart—and with it, his spiritual sensitivity. We knew that if we didn't help identify and bear Jasha's personal burdens, he would have to bear them alone. That would have tempted him not to trust his heavenly Father to bear his burdens. And if God could not bear his burdens, Jasha might have concluded that God could not bear the weight of the world's burdens without his constant assistance. In the end, he might have become even more like the overburdened people I have just described.

We also recognized that no matter how long or hard Jasha cried, he wasn't feeling any better. So we plopped down on either side of him on our comfy couch, stretched our arms around him, and asked him to lean into us. After helping him put words to his anguish, we asked, "Jasha, during all the times you tried to comfort others, what did you do with your own hurts?" He replied, "I guess I just stuffed them down." And with a heave, he broke into a few more sobs. But this time, he let us bear *his* burdens, and he felt comforted in ways he had never felt before. That day, Jasha agreed to forgive us for times we were unable to comfort each other enough to keep him from thinking he had to take over our job. We lifted away a few pounds of his lifelong accumulation of burdens. Jasha soon came to the end of his tears. That night and from then on, he slept more soundly than he had in many years.

If I hadn't received enough healing myself, I would fret about the multitudes of tender souls who have never heard of the healing tools Carol offers in this book, and who aren't even aware that what they (or their children) are experiencing is not just their own inexplicable woe. But I have taken a few steps toward learning to trust God to carry all the Jasha's of the world. Therefore, I am learning to let God give me my assignments; He enables me to help just a few select souls bear their burdens to the cross.

...Lord, grant me the faith to leave the rest with you.

That faith is helped by the knowledge that this book is in the hands of beleaguered burden bearers. The principles it covers enable me to trust that you, and the rest of the entire beleaguered world, are in the hands of the only One who truly is strong enough to bear the crushing weight upon His shoulders.

Mark Sanford
Elijah House Ministries

Introduction

S ELF-HELP BOOKS, CODEPENDENCY TEACHINGS, AND recovery groups tell you that you are responsible for making your own feelings. They say no one else can "make" you feel a certain way; rather, it is a fault of your own thinking patterns. It is good and important to learn to take responsibility, but what if you have done everything you can to be responsible for "your own stuff" and still feel deep uncontrollable unease, anger, or other feelings? What more can you do? Welcome to the ongoing quest to make sense of life—to find meaning to the odd and confusing thoughts and emotions that seem to come from "nowhere!"

You can easily become overwhelmed by the continual flow of sensory data. This book was written to help you rein life in so that it becomes more manageable. I talk about how to sort through the confusing jumble of "stuff" to figure out what is your own feeling, your own sore growth spot, from all that continually bombards you, and how to identify what of all that is a burden God wants you to carry to the cross. Learning how to discern these differences is a huge lesson, and it is essential if you are to thrive as a highly sensitive Christian, rather than just survive.

In *Highly Sensitive: Understanding Your Gift of Spiritual Sensitivity*, you will find hope and encouragement in regard to hearing God. If you do not have confidence in your hearing, you may find help in the chapters on Hearing From God and Blocks to Hearing. I admit that it is difficult to hear God when the enemy has you by both ears!

I also talk about how to learn to not be so hard on yourself. You have been highly sensitive, a burden bearer, all your life, so learning to bring intuitive responses to consciousness will be a process. Jesus is the master burden bearer—you and I are apprentices. You are learning a language, a spiritual language—and that takes time. Learning means that you will not do it right the first time or all the time! And that is OK! The world will not stop spinning, and those you love will not self destruct if you "do not do it right" or miss it altogether.

Do you feel like everyone else's agenda is worked on, but never yours? You try to finish a task, but are continually interrupted because their problems need attention *now*! How do you stop people and life from overwhelming you? You will also find help with that in this book.

If you have spent your life being the family's emotional dumping ground or steam vent, if you have been told that you are too sensitive and you better toughen up, if you have been called crazy, a basket case, and so forth, if you have been mocked, dismissed, minimized, or rejected, after a while, you begin to believe and agree with what others say about you. You begin to see yourself the way others describe you. Your reaction is to "not want to be this way" and to shut off the incoming emotion—if only you could! How you see and feel about yourself has a great deal to do with how you come to God and what you believe He can and will do *because **you** ask Him to!* If you are to thrive rather than just survive as a highly sensitive burden bearer, you need to build or repair some inner structures. This book will help you do that.

The companion volume to this one, *The Mystery of Spiritual Sensitivity*, explains the concept of burden bearing and how highly sensitive people can experience *other people's* emotions as their own! I describe how sensitive people are often misunderstood and mocked for being "too sensitive;" their feelings are dismissed or rejected. *The Mystery of Spiritual Sensitivity* identifies the real reason for some of your out-of-control emotions and gives practical tips for understanding yourself and prayer models to guide you into receiving God's healing and help. He did not design you this way to make you crazy, but to give you information for prayer—empathetic, burden bearing prayer! As a highly sensitive burden bearer, He invites you to partner with Him in His ongoing ministry of reconciliation. God takes on Himself the responsibility to do for you what you cannot do—things like salvation, healing, and sanctification. However, He will *not* do for you what you can and need to do for yourself—like learning, developing, and maturing.

The Mystery of Spiritual Sensitivity was gratefully received by people who otherwise had started to wonder if everyone else was right and maybe there *was* something wrong with the way they were made. I received many thanks for the book; check out some of the testimonies on my Website! If you have not read *The Mystery of Spiritual Sensitivity*, don't put this book down! I have included enough summary for you to understand the concept of burden bearing and how it works. You will still benefit from reading this volume. At some point you will want to read the other one as well for a fuller understanding.

Highly Sensitive: Understanding Your Gift of Spiritual Sensitivity is in response to the loud and frequently asked questions, "But what do I do now? Where do I go from here? Can I learn to live with this gift before it kills me?" In it you will find guidelines for how to live as an overcoming "burden bearer" instead of being controlled and overwhelmed by other's needs. While *The Mystery of Spiritual Sensitivity* helped you discern your true identity and receive God's healing, *Highly Sensitive: Understanding Your Gift of Spiritual Sensitivity* focuses on the spiritual habits and disciplines you can develop to cooperate with God's plan for you—the learning, maturing, and developing. The two books can be read in any order.

Seeing life as a time of preparation is a comfort to me. Like Queen Esther, you will be presented to the King one day. This life is about learning how to walk, talk, live, and love like Jesus. And if you are highly sensitive, burden bearing may be the spiritual workout regimen that molds and sculpts you into a striking resemblance of Jesus. My prayer is that reading this book will help you understand yourself better, be kinder to yourself, and implement specific and practical things you can do as you cooperate with God to heal and restructure your inner being! Some chapters lend themselves to more in-depth meditation and personal work with the Lord. For those chapters, I designed worksheets which you may download free from my Website: www.fromGodsheart.com. (Click "The Book" tab.)

I was 40 before I learned about burden bearing. What a relief that was! Life does not have to be burdensome. You do not have to endure life as a joyless existence, simply hanging on until eventually God calls you home! Be encouraged—there is hope and meaning. Jesus will take you at your word when you ask Him to be in charge of your sensitivity. That puts Him in the driver's seat, so buckle your seat belts! He doesn't slow down on the learning curve—and it is a doozie! Hang on and enjoy the ride!

Blessings,
Carol

CHAPTER 1

Welcome to My World

MYSTIFIED, **S**TEPHEN **STOOD LOOKING AT** Mirianna, his wife.[1] "You are killing me! You are killing me!" she yelled. The comfortable, peaceful, little cottage suddenly became electric. He could feel the bubble of joy that had buoyed him all the way home slowly deflate, punctured by her words. Thoughts tumbled about in his head, but he said nothing; his face twisted with grief.

What could you possibly mean? he thought. *You are the love of my life, my world. You give meaning to everything I do. To share life with you is all I want. I could never hurt you, and yet, here I am obviously hurting you, and I don't know how—or why!*

He took a step toward her, but Mirianna shrank back, avoiding his touch as if it would hurt. She knew he only wanted to comfort her, but she could not allow him near her—not yet. She could feel the pain she caused by shrinking back, which added to the overwhelming amount she already felt coming from him. An inarticulate sound of anguish escaped as Stephen turned and went outside. He would walk—five miles maybe, and talk with his Lord. Mirianna would be more like herself, at least able to talk, when he returned. Homecoming from every conference or convention was this way. Why, he had no idea, but he did not like it. He wanted to share his joy with his beautiful, sensitive, loving mate. Joy always multiplied in the sharing. That is what he desired to give it to her, and then they would both have joy—twice the joy! The last thing he wanted was for the joy to escape into the atmosphere and disappear!

Mirianna was the center of Stephen's world, but Jesus was the center of his universe. Nothing gave him more joy than to work with his Lord, repairing the saints (see Eph. 4:12). His life was to serve his Lord by bringing hurting people together with those who could help and encourage. He organized conferences and conventions regionally and nationally, wherever people needed them. The multitude of details challenged him. He loved to see people helped and healed; it energized him to see God work! To not love and serve either his Lord or his wife was unthinkable. It would literally tear him apart; at least that is how he felt at the moment.

The inarticulate sound that Stephen made as he turned to walk off the burdens of the conference was a prayer. Scripture says that the Spirit makes intercession with groanings that cannot be uttered (see Rom. 8:26). The Lord understood what Stephen's spirit was saying! It was a prayer of invitation to come into the situation, to carry the heavy end of this painful burden. Now it was the Lord's turn to organize people and circumstances.

That was how Stephen came to attend the international school on prayer ministry where my husband David and I were teaching. Earlier in the day, David broke with the planned program, sensing from the Lord that my talk about burden bearing was more important for this group than the one scheduled.

It was break time now, and 150-200 people milled about the cavernous, old church. Light streamed through beautiful, tall stained glass windows. Little groups of people chatted and stretched. Other folks needed coffee. I joined that line and wondered why the cup was only half-full—but after one taste, I too reached for the cream and sugar to top off the cup! I sipped the hot corrosive liquid and watched as one of the pastors purposefully made his way in my direction. I had noticed him before. He was of average height and weight, had round, rosy cheeks, and needed a haircut, like most of the men in attendance! He was one of the Energizer Bunnies—going, going, going! What I liked most about him was the laugh wrinkles around his eyes and mouth. They testified to the joy and good humor with which he lived his life.

As he neared me, his eyes began to dance and set the laugh wrinkles in motion. He reached out and grabbed my hand with both of his. "Thank you, thank you, *and thank you*. You have given me my wife back!" The dancing eyes misted, and his voice cracked with emotion as he relayed the story you just read.

He continued. "Now I understand. I did not know that if I do not pass on to the Lord what I feel in others, the spiritual and emotional pain, confusion, and trouble could cling to me like cigarette smoke! I brought it into the house with me so *it felt* to my wife like I was causing her pain. She is so sensitive that even the echo of other people's pain, the residue on me, was enough to feel like I was killing her." He paused and shook his head.

"During that five-mile walk, as I poured out my heart to Jesus, the Holy Spirit was drawing the pain from the conference right on through me to the cross! The five-mile walk was my "spiritual shower!" That was why Mirianna was *"more like herself"* when I came back! *I* was different; *I* was clean. For the first time, I understand my wife! Thank you. Now I know I must do the "cleansing prayer" you talked about before I arrive at home. Thank you." He walked away a happy man.

Before the Lord took me on the "burden bearing" learning curve, I experienced life as a continual, oppressive weight that never let up. I turned to God with it—where else do you go? People did not understand. Doctors said, "You are healthy, fine; there is nothing wrong with you!" Yet, I knew something was dreadfully wrong. I was so tired that I cried out to God for permission to have a nervous breakdown. "Please let me crack so I can go to the hospital and sleep for a few months!"

I heard the Lord's response very clearly. "No, you will never have a nervous breakdown. Your mind is too strong."

At the time, those words of assurance did not comfort me. They felt very cold. He did not abandon me; He still talked to me, but I *felt* alone and in a very dark place. I wished He did not think I could endure so much or think I was so strong. I knew the everlasting arms were underneath—I just did not know how far down. Nor did David, my husband, know that being the pastor meant that he, and therefore I, would wear the burdens of the congregation as if they were our own! Unredeemed burden bearing is actually doing the work of the spirit with the strength of the soul. My body and soul cannot carry that much—no one's can.

You see, unredeemed burden bearing *can* kill you. Mirianna knew it, and so did I. We did not know *what* was killing us, only that "something" was. Residue of burdens not discharged builds up inside you the way freezing rain builds ice on a tree until limbs break. Eventually, you break at your weakest link. Rather than tell you what unredeemed burden bearing is, let me tell you about redeemed burden bearing—doing it the way God designed us to do it. But to draw a full picture, you need some background.

WHAT IS BURDEN BEARING?

Burden bearing is the prayer response to the feelings, emotions, and spiritual content you sense in another individual when the Holy Spirit connects you empathetically. It is responding to God's call or nudge or prompting to come alongside an individual in an overwhelming situation. As you sense what the individual is experiencing and pray, the Holy Spirit draws some of that burden through you onto the Cross of Jesus. The person is able to function. His mind clears; with the mind clear she can see options she could not see before, and pray her own prayers.

This does not mean that you and I bear other people's burdens in precisely the same way that Christ does, for He is the only mediator between God and people who can offer us salvation (see 1 Tim. 2:5). But we are privileged to help draw others toward His saving work: *"All this is from God, who reconciled us to Himself through Christ and **gave us the ministry of reconciliation"** (2 Cor. 5:18). In this book, when I speak of bearing another's sin to the cross, I am not speaking of that work which is exclusively Christ's.

I do believe that there are times when we are called to "repent" on behalf of others, as did Nehemiah: *"...I confess the sins **we** Israelites...have committed against you"* (Neh. 1:6). However, this is not a saving repentance, nor one that transforms the hearts of those for whom we intercede. Rather, we place the cross between the people for whom we intercede and the full consequences of their sins. For instance, when the people grumbled against Moses about the dangers of entering the Promised Land, God threatened to destroy them. But when Moses asked God to forgive them, God replied, "I have forgiven them, as you asked," and He did not destroy them (see Num. 14:20).

This principle has carried over to the New Testament. When Stephen was stoned, he pleaded, *"Do not hold this sin against them..."* (Acts. 7:60). And First John 5:16 says, *"If anyone sees his brother commit a sin that does not lead to death, he should pray and God will give him life...."* Although we cannot save our brother in the sense that only Christ can, we can prevent him from reaping harm and enable him to receive the life that his sin would otherwise prevent him from receiving. This can encourage and empower our brother to choose to come to his own repentance.

As burden bearers, we are also privileged to suffer with Christ for others. Once again, this is not in the saving way that Christ, our only mediator, suffered. But in other ways we can share in the fellowship of His sufferings (see Phil. 3:10). We can *"mourn with those who mourn"* (Rom. 12:15). We can be like Paul who asked, *"Who is weak, and I do not feel weak?"* (2 Cor.11:29a). By feeling with others, we can lift the load of pain that one person alone cannot bear. We can carry this to the cross, leaving her with a lighter load, thus enabling her to embrace the Holy Spirit as Comforter. As burden bearers, we do this by the ability to synchronize with others combined with the spiritual gifts of word of knowledge (see 1 Cor. 12:8), mercy (see Rom. 12:8), and sometimes prophecy (see 1 Cor. 12:10); the Holy Spirit enables us to simply "know" another's hidden and unspoken pain and mercifully pray it off of her weary shoulders.

This kind of "burden bearing" is a form of intercession that begins in the heart of God. You are able to pray intelligently and specifically into someone's situation because, *by empathy,* you have felt what he experiences. Empathy is "receptivity to the sensory and emotional experiences of another to the point that you feel what they are experiencing."[2] This is not extra-sensory perception (ESP). Scripture is quite clear that God speaks to His people in 1 Corinthians 12 and Job 33:13-14.

Burden bearing is possible because of three things: your ability to empathize (with people and God), the work of Jesus on the Cross, and the work of the Holy Spirit. The burden forms in the heart of God as He sees a need in someone's life. Rather than barge in and fix the problem, He respects a person's free will and asks you, His servant, to be part of His solution. He wants you to be the *person through whom* He draws the pain of a hurting person to Himself. He asks you to be His hands on earth to relieve physical suffering and to stand for Him as an emissary of comfort and freedom from emotional and spiritual bondage.

To this end He designed your body, not only to be an instrument of praise, but of prayer. He designed you and me to be sensitive, some more highly so than others. This kind of "burden bearing" involves the body, the emotions, and the senses all working together. This God-given sensitivity allows you to connect with people on all levels—physical, emotional, psychological, and spiritual. Galatians 6:2 commands that we *"carry* [or bear] *each other's burdens, and in this way you will fulfill the law of Christ."* That law, of course, is that we *"love one another as I* [Jesus] *have loved you..."* (John 13:34). I don't know about you, but I am unwilling to set my life aside for others if I feel nothing of their struggle, their pain! When I feel their pain, compassion moves me to come alongside to lighten their load.

I believe burden bearing is a major part of what the apostle Paul was talking about when he said, *"Now I rejoice in what was suffered for you, and I fill up in my flesh what is still lacking in regard to Christ's afflictions, for the sake of His body, which is the church"* (Col. 1:24). Elsewhere he says, *"Who is weak, and I do not feel weak?"* (2 Cor.

11:29a). Empathy is key. Without empathy, you cannot sense the heart of God where burden bearing originates.

BURDEN BEARING IS NOT ESP

Sometimes God speaks audibly. For such cases, He built us with physical ears to hear Him. But usually He speaks inaudibly. For those times, He built us with spiritual ears. It is not evil to have such "ears." But it is indeed evil to turn them toward any other source than the Holy Spirit.

Turning spiritual ears toward a source other than the Holy Spirit is called extra-sensory perception (ESP). ESP is using God-given abilities without the boundaries and protection of the Holy Spirit. In the use of these abilities, a "spirit" may aid some, without their knowing; others consciously *use* a spirit other than God. Dependence upon a source other than God is what you are not to do. No one cares for you more than God. He knows what is in your best interest. Such dependence on other spirits is an open door for the forces of darkness. *Such use of high sensitivity is divination.*

Scripture is clear that believers are not to be involved in such practices (see Deut. 18:10,14; 1 Sam. 15:23; 2 Chron. 33:6). The Oxford Dictionary defines divination as "the art or practice of obtaining hidden knowledge from supernatural powers" other than God.[3] The Merriam-Webster online dictionary gives a second definition: "insight; intuitive perception."[4] These are apt descriptions of the way that *kosem* (the Hebrew word for "divination" in Deuteronomy 18) was practiced in Bible times. Here the English and Hebrew definitions harmonize. I would add to that definition by saying that it is unusual insight and intuitive perception without God's authorization or protection. In other words, peering where not invited out of curiosity, seeking status, control, or personal gain—such as in fortune telling, tarot cards, ouija boards, séances, and so forth. God does not endorse such practices.

Burden bearing is different from ESP or clairvoyance because burden bearing rightly means complete surrender to God of your ability to see, sense, and feel. You ask the Lord to be in charge of it in you and to only let you see or feel or sense at the direction of the Holy Spirit through His gifts, such as mercy (see Rom. 12:8) and word of knowledge (see 1 Cor. 12:8—in this case, supernaturally receiving from the Holy Spirit knowledge of what another feels) and direction for how to pray about what you have been given. Your abilities are "crucified and resurrected" and harnessed to God's will. It is no longer you who is doing this work, but the Holy Spirit in you. The Holy Spirit is central to bearing burdens rightly. Without the Holy Spirit, bearing burdens rightly does not happen.

The Holy Spirit uses your resurrected and redeemed ability to empathize and connects you with those who need His love, help, and healing touch. At the Holy Spirit's direction, you feel their pain. That pain alerts you to another's needs and informs your prayer so that you will accurately and compassionately invite the Lord to aid or heal the hurting person. Like a neural synapse in the brain, the Holy Spirit forms a "spiritual synapse" from a hurting person to one who can help lighten the load.

Some misguided highly sensitive people sincerely want to help in whatever way they can. In response to the inner directive to lighten people's loads, they "help" through psychic means. Psychics are highly sensitive people who have not met and surrendered to Jesus. Some, when they are introduced to Jesus, happily receive Him and His salvation, protection, and wisdom, and they renounce all psychic practices. Others not only fall into such practices, but seek them out and try to develop more. They do not realize that the power comes with a price and that one day satan will require the loan to be paid back with horrendous interest! "Special" knowledge gives them a sense of power, control, status, and/or monetary gain. For some, the need to belong is so powerful that they choose to ignore the fact that the power they think they are wielding actually controls, manipulates, and abuses them.

What would burden bearing look like, done rightly? I could cite Mother Theresa, Rees Howells, or the apostle Paul—but a more "everyday" example would be my friend Colleen who awoke to what she thought was arthritis in her hands. Arthritis has a strong genetic presence in her family, so she figured it was her turn, her destiny—until she remembered our conversation the night before. She lifted her hands toward Heaven and asked, "Lord, whose hands are these?" A woman's face came to mind. Colleen prayed for her, asking the Lord to comfort those hands. She could pray intelligently and passionately—she *knew* how it felt! Shortly the pain in her hands was gone. She did not have arthritis! The Lord connected her to someone who did; she empathized with the woman's pain and asked her heavenly Father's help. Later that day she called this woman and asked about her hands. She learned that the pain had subsided at the very time Colleen prayed—and it did not come back!

Although Colleen experienced some temporary discomfort, bearing another person's pain to the cross caused her no lasting harm. The wave of God's healing and comfort washed over Colleen on its way to the person for whom she prayed. She was cleansed and her friend was comforted. Both women were encouraged. Their faith grew. Their confidence in God's caring concern grew. The relationship between the two women was stronger! The benefits of less than an hour of discomfort went out like ripples on a pond. This is what burden bearing does, and more, when submitted to the lordship of Jesus! If Colleen had not prayed, my conviction is that the arthritis would have stayed in her hands!

Have you been described as ultra or overly sensitive? If you have, I believe you were designed to be that way by God. Research tells us that approximately 20-30 percent of the population in general is wired in this different way.[5] The central nervous system of highly sensitive people is designed to read and draw in more data than the rest of the population. This design is a variation on the theme of "normal;" it is not wrong, just different. However, when you are different from most of the people around you, you can feel as if you are wrong. Many others are happy to tell you what you are—that you are weird, overly sensitive, too emotional, and so forth. The lack of acceptance for who you are, how you are made, and how you express yourself can lead to a poor self-image, low self-esteem, and a distrust of your own perceptions.

Another perspective is that you are like finely-tuned radar that senses and reads nuances that most miss. Thus, without meaning to, you hear more than the words people say. You sense and feel what may be going on below the level of other peoples' consciousness, physically, emotionally, or spiritually. If this natural sensitivity is not submitted to the cross of Christ, it can lead you into occult or New Age practices that are forbidden by Scripture. But when you allow your sensitive nature to die with Christ on His cross, He can focus your hearing on Him alone and gift you with the gifts of His Spirit (see 1 Cor. 12).

Additionally, God built into the human design the ability to be corporate—to, in some sensory way, experience what other people feel. The first part of your brain that comes on line after you are born is dedicated to reading others' emotions and emotional states and doing your own emoting emotions. You might say that the cingulate cortex is where empathy resides. Empathy makes it possible to be a responsible member of a family, group, tribe, and so forth. It is your first language. This part of your brain communicates directly with its counterpart in other individuals so that you adjust and match their internal state within 90 seconds! You really *can* feel someone's pain! The cingulate cortex also works in conjunction with your human spirit, making it possible to connect with the heart of God in the same way that you can connect with other people.

Empathy is for the emotions what your words and speech mechanism are for the mind. It is the certain something that connects you with others. The essence of empathy is sensitivity, and the essence of burden bearing is empathy—empathy for others and empathy with God. Being able to sense God's heart means being grieved by what grieves God, being devastated by what devastates Him. It means rejoicing with those who rejoice (see Rom. 12:15) and sensing the pleasure God feels when His children please or honor Him. Coming alongside people in trouble and helping to carry their overwhelming, crushing load to the cross pleases and honors your loving Lord. Bearing another person's burden to the cross is imitating Jesus. God spoke from Heaven saying, *"This is My Son, whom I love; with Him I am well pleased"* (Matt. 3:16-17). He was very pleased with Jesus, and He is pleased with those who live and love like Jesus.

There is only one mediator between God and man (see 1 Tim. 2:5), so you and I cannot bear others' sins in the same way Jesus does. But we do share in Jesus' sufferings (see Phil. 3:10) by weeping with those who weep (see Rom. 12:15) and by helping to bear their burdens. *"Carry* [bear] *one another's burdens and in this way you will fulfill the law of Christ"* (Gal. 6:2).

Unfortunately, contemporary culture does not teach you about your corporate nature. Because you lack this information, you probably assume that everything you feel is yours. Since highly sensitive people comprise only 20-30 percent of the population, 70-80 percent are less sensitive and extend varying degrees of graciousness or understanding to the highly sensitive.

Misunderstanding and less than gracious responses are hurtful, so you learn to cope. You build homemade armor to protect yourself from further hurt. Homemade armor does not fit properly or protect completely (as the spiritual armor that God provides does), but as a child, stinging from the hurt of rejection, minimization, mockery, or dismissal, you did not know that. You protected yourself because you did not see anyone else helping. You will find a full explanation of this armor and the problems it causes in Chapter Four of the prequel to this book, *The Mystery of Spiritual Sensitivity*.[6]

The most devastating thing is that hurt from misunderstanding puts a wedge between you and your God-given design. You quickly try "not to be like that;" you try to shut down your sensitivity. Each hurt increases the degree of turning from who God made you to be. Satan quickly puts a wedge in your relationship with God. He whispers, "Why is God not helping? Why is He not protecting? Why is He not making things better?" And on and on. You learn not to trust your own perceptions or those of the ones who "love" you, and you learn not to trust God.

REACTIONS TO SENSITIVITY

People with a highly sensitive design tend to have one of two reactions to their sensitivity. The first is to follow the intuitive directive to "help make things better." They throw themselves into fixing whatever and whomever they sense needs fixing or helping. Fixing and helping beyond what God authorizes moves them into unredeemed burden bearing—carrying that which God has not given them to carry. The second tendency is to withdraw because there is too much pain out there. Those who withdraw have concluded that trying to help make things better is an exercise in futility! They simply try to remove themselves from the source of pain—people!

PLANS FOR YOUR LIFE

Satan's plan is to turn you from the Lord and to manipulate you into hating the way you are made. If he can turn you from your design, he hurts God's heart. He will do that by tempting you to either turn off your sensitivity or to use it in occult ways forbidden by Scripture. He wants to get back at God—he does not give a flying fig about you or me except that hurting us is the most effective way to hurt God.

God's plan is to reconcile all humankind to Himself—to completely undo the mischief satan made by causing the Fall in the Garden of Eden. He includes in this ministry of reconciliation all Christians who are willing to participate. Highly sensitive people are uniquely designed with the kind of sensitivity that makes them receptive to the Holy Spirit's discernment, which enables them to sense God's desires, to sense people's needs, to feel their pain, and to use that information to cry out intelligently and passionately to God and invite Him to come help. This is what Paul was talking about in Galatians 6:2: *"Carry each other's burdens, and in this way you will fulfill the law of Christ."* Carrying each other's burdens is what I am referring to when I use the phrase *burden bearing*. You and I need to learn how to do this only in God's power so that we are not overwhelmed or overburdened—we need to do it in a joy-filled way that allows us to thrive *with* the gift!

All Christians are *commanded* to bear burdens. Look at the language in Galatians 6:2—there are no qualifiers, no loopholes. Everyone will be called upon, at some time, to help bear others' overwhelming loads so that they can function and their minds can be clear, so they can have their own thoughts, pray their own prayers, and see their options. Highly sensitive people are uniquely designed to sense and know when help is needed! They find themselves involved in this form of intercession more than most people.

Burden bearing is a form of intercession that begins in the heart of God. Other forms of intercession begin when you see needs and plead others' cases before the Lord. With burden bearing, He sees someone in trouble, a situation going from bad to worse, and He uses you to help. The problem is, He gave people free will and has not changed His mind about it. He does not impose, but waits to intervene until invited. But when people are overwhelmed, they forget that He wants to help. They forget to ask for help; they simply try to survive. That is when our loving Father taps on the shoulder of a burden bearer and shares His grief over the person in trouble. He may share His grief with you by downloading it directly into your spirit. He may draw you to interact with the individual, or He may bring that person's name or face to your mind as a way to call you to pray.

How It Works

The Lord connects your spirit to the spirit of the hurting one.

An exchange is made between you and the hurting one—some of the Lord's life, joy, and happiness is in you for that person's burden. You turn to the Lord with the burden and ask, "What is this? For whom do you want me to pray?" You discern the "who" or "what" and then take time to feel as much of that burden as God wills. You let what you sense and feel inform a prayer for that individual, group, or situation. You can pray intelligently and specifically because you feel what that person experiences. You can pour your heart out to God with passion when you feel something intensely.

If the "who" and "what" does not become clear, you allow yourself to sense and feel the grief God shares with you. What you sense and feel informs the prayer you pray, inviting Him to do what is in His heart. The Holy Spirit finds every place where the burden has settled in you, gathers it, and lifts it up, out, and off of you as you pray. The Holy Spirit in you puts that burden on the cross of Jesus, and from there it is Jesus' responsibility. But that is not the end!

Father God responds. He wants to help. Now that you have invited Him to act on behalf of this individual, He can do what was in His heart to do in the first place. He releases healing, love, life, comfort—whatever He knows is needed. He may arrange people and circumstances so this person can have a divine encounter!

A wave of healing love flows from the heart of God and washes over you on its way to the individual you just prayed for. It cleanses, refreshes, and comforts your heart. Often you need some healing and cleansing after being loaded up with someone else's trouble, confusion, sin, or pain! The Lord restores the life, joy, and happiness that was yours before that "exchange" took place. He replaces it with interest!

Burden bearers who have a tendency to be "fixers" often want to do more than God requires, to carry responsibility for the person or situation. The same Scripture that urges us to *carry one another's burdens"* (Gal. 6:2), goes on to say, *"For each one should carry his own load"* (Gal. 6:5). Letting go is difficult—there is a subconscious fear that God might not respond or not respond "right," and somehow it will "be my fault." However, your job is finished when you discharge the burden at the cross. If the Lord does not directly ask you to do something else, you should not. Emotions sometimes pull you to help beyond what God authorizes. God supplies the strength to do what He calls you to do. He does not necessarily supply the strength needed for your "good ideas!" Burden bearers driven by undisciplined compassion spread themselves thin and wear themselves out. Undisciplined compassion does not have the wisdom, strength, or direction of the Holy Spirit. Here is a principle: undisciplined compassion leads to burnout! Burned out burden bearers are no good to themselves, God, or others. Everyone loses, which is what satan wants.

Going ahead of God, helping Him out—carrying too many burdens, carrying them too long—is unredeemed burden bearing. It is bearing burdens in your own strength and trying to do the work of the Holy Spirit with the strength of your soul. You may bring the individual temporary relief, but the Lord desires the lasting fix.

Burdens not given to you by God or not discharged at the cross of Jesus sit in your body, mind, and spirit. If the burden is similar to an unhealed sore spot of your own, it will sit on top of your own emotions and intensify, amplify, and exaggerate what you feel. An unhealed "sore spot" can be any area you do not want to visit, be it from physical, emotional, or spiritual wounds. Burdens will also aggravate physical weaknesses.

I know a woman who is prone to headaches whenever her life becomes tense. She is also highly sensitive, so if God calls her to pray for an individual who is overburdened with tension, it compounds her own tension and brings on a headache or makes the one she has more painful. One might ask if this means she is not really called to do this intercession. But I know her well enough to discern that her call is true. God is using her struggles to reveal areas in her heart where she has not yet trusted Him so that He can heal those areas. Thus, in the long run, burden bearing is bringing her closer to a place where she will be tension free!

Accumulated burdens may reveal or bring underlying propensities to the surface. I cannot cite you a medical study, but here is my logic. We catch colds when we are over busy and do not have adequate sleep. Medical literature and my doctor tell me that we all carry "cold bugs" in our bodies all the time. The immune system is usually able to keep them at bay. However, when we overtax our systems by exposure to someone with a cold or by requiring too much from our bodies, a cold often surfaces.

Burden bearing in your own strength overtaxes your body's ability to keep you healthy in the same way. It puts stresses on the body that you were not designed to bear. Stress is your body's archenemy. Your immune system cannot keep up the battle against foreign invaders indefinitely *and* cope with continually accumulating stress from burden bearing in your own strength. Underlying, dormant propensities may present themselves sooner than they would have otherwise. Doctors do say that excessive stress wears you down. Your weakest link gives way.

God designed your body with a central nervous system and a cingulate cortex that is dedicated to emotion—to emoting and to monitoring, moderating, and modulating emotions. He designed you with the capacity to empathize. In cooperation with the Holy Spirit, through prayer, because of Jesus' work on the cross, your ability to empathize makes it possible to *divide* sorrow and *multiply* joy. Unredeemed burden bearing *adds* to the sorrow and *subtracts* from the joy. This dynamic occurs in all relationships, but is especially true with married couples.

Burdens ping-pong between the couple. Unbidden by God, the wife reaches out in her human spirit to draw down her husband's burden or to lift his heaviness, but without bearing the burden to the cross. By reflex, the husband, sensing the added weight, tries to draw down the pain of his wife (and vice versa). Each time this happens (when the burden is not taken to the Lord), they each add to their own heaviness. The tension grows until one or the other abruptly ends the interchange or says something that will be regretted later—like, "You care more about work than you do about your family!" In this case, burden bearing did not facilitate intimacy and unity, the very thing that it is designed to do!

How burden bearing works within marriage and with parenting is the subject of two long chapters in *The Mystery of Spiritual Sensitivity*. Other subjects discussed are life complications (areas of vulnerability that are part of the package of being highly sensitive), the blessings of burden bearing, and how to bring healing for hurts because of being highly sensitive and incurred in burden bearing. There is an entire chapter devoted to sample prayers for healing. This short explanation of what burden bearing is and how it works should give you enough background to benefit from reading this book without having read *The Mystery of Spiritual Sensitivity*. However, you will want to read it so that your understanding is more complete.

What was God thinking when He made some of us so highly sensitive? Knowing the full mind of God is another mystery beyond our design capabilities! The story in Genesis suggests that the three persons of the Godhead (Father, Son, and Holy Spirit) so enjoyed their relationship that creating more beings in their own image would be joy upon joy for them. God created humankind for relationship with Him. God wanted more children then, and He still does. Salvation achieves that goal. However, you and I are in a bit of a mess and hardly prepared for our ultimate destiny as sons or daughters of the King, as co-heirs ruling and reigning with Jesus. Hanging out with Jesus bearing burdens, becoming dirty and sweaty, wrestling with the trouble, pain, and confusion that sin brings, will develop your relationship with Him as nothing else can. It works the character and nature of Jesus into you. You begin to sound like Him, live like Him, and love like Him. Burden bearing is a participatory activity—you working *with* God reconciling people to Him, each other, and themselves.

Part of burden bearing is God's domain, and part is your domain. *The Mystery of Spiritual Sensitivity* is primarily about God's domain, what He did and does for you and your reactions. I wrote it to give voice and vocabulary to how you experience life, to give you hope and comfort as well as understanding of how the Lord designed you to bear burdens. You are not crazy, but you are different from many—and that is a good thing!

Highly Sensitive: Understanding Your Gift of Spiritual Sensitivity is about your domain—about the things you can choose to work on under God's direction. It is about spiritual fitness—building in the structures, habits, and disciplines that will enable you to do the good works that were designed for you to do from the beginning (see Eph. 2:10). Many people are conscious of health and fitness and work out faithfully. You are much more than your body; you also need to tend to spiritual fitness. This life is, in some respects, a marathon. You need to acquire knowledge and expertise, develop stamina and perseverance, if you are to run this race with joy (see Heb. 12:1). This book is about the issues highly sensitive people wrestle with and the inner structures you need to build to live a joy-filled life as a burden bearer, before the "gift" kills you!

Your learning curve is going to go up at nearly a 90-degree angle. The angle will not be so steep after a while, but for now, fasten your seat belts. Jesus is driving! As you allow Him, He will draw you into situations and circumstances that can teach and train you how to bear burdens in a redeemed fashion—so it does not wear you out—so that you will not feel like it is killing you. He will work the character and nature of Jesus into you so you can walk with joy into your destiny as a son or daughter of the King and as a co-heir with Jesus.

Once *The Mystery of Spiritual Sensitivity* was in reader's hands, the loudest questions I heard were, "Now what? Where do I go from here?" This volume attempts to answer those questions. The following chapters deal with your domain. These are issues you can work on—issues of *your* personal development and maturation. Jesus will help you, but He will not do the work for you. Each of you is unique, so He will arrange individual learning experiences tailor-made for you. Yet, as a group, burden bearers share the "big five":

- Difficulty hearing God or recognizing that you do hear Him

- Difficulty discerning between someone else's burden and your own

- Boundaries

- Trust

- Issues of identity

As you embrace burden bearing as a lifestyle, engage the struggle to change, take the risks of relationships, and develop the disciplines He assigns you, with God's guidance and empowerment, you will develop a more striking resemblance to Jesus.

ENDNOTES

1. Fictional names.

2. Carol Brown, *The Mystery of Spiritual Sensitivity* (Shippensburg, PA: Destiny Image, 2008), p. 28.

3. Oxford Dictionary, 10th Edition, Oxford 4.

4. Elaine Aron, *Highly Sensitive Person* (New York: Broadway Books, 1998), p. xiv of preface.

5. Carol Brown, *The Mystery of Spiritual Sensitivity* (Shippensburg, PA: Destiny Image, 2008), p. 75-114.

CHAPTER 2

How We Learn

IMAGINE, IF YOU WILL, YOUNG King David, barely cleaned up from his extended stay in "the Outback" with the sheep, when his dad sends him off to the frontlines with supplies for the older brothers. As he approaches the battlefield, he hears some rude Philistine hurling insults and mocking the soldiers and God. At first he is in shock at the way this pagan assaults the reputation of the God he has come to know and love. Then he is incredulous that the king and the soldiers have done nothing about it! Day after day they listen to this heathen assassinate the character of God as well as call the soldiers' lineage and parentage into question. Dumbfounded, David blurts out his sentiments without thinking. The next thing he knows, someone has slapped Saul's armour on him! He can't walk, let alone run. The helmet is too large; it slips down over one eye, and he can hardly see. The sword and shield are big and clumsy. The chest armour hits him on the knees. David says, "Um, fellas, I can't fight like this!"

Your eyes are opened as you come to understand burden bearing and receive some healing from the related wounds sustained in childhood. Still, you realize the helmet of salvation is over one eye. Your flak jacket of righteousness is unzipped. The shield of faith and the sword of truth are banging about, nicking and cutting legs and ankles—yours included! The girdle of truth pinches, and you are stepping on people's toes with the hobnailed boots of peace! You can't be a soldier for Christ like this! You can't build the Kingdom—you can't *live* like this!

You are in the same pickle David was in—wearing unfamiliar body armor and trying to use tools you aren't trained to use. David spent many an hour plinking rocks at bushes, trees, and little critters, some of which he later cooked for supper. He knew how to use a sling. In time he learned to use the weapons of warfare that Saul was so eager for him to wield, but only in time. David had to grow into his armour. You too have to become familiar with and *learn* to use the equipment you have been given. As you come into an understanding of burden bearing, you realize that you've had a sling in your back pocket all along. You need to learn how to wind up, take aim, and release. You especially need to know *what* to aim at! A novice slingshot artist would not do well letting fly at a bear unless he knew what to do when the bear charged. It is important for you to know when to "let fly" with prayer and when to call in the "spiritual cavalry" to fight battles for which you are unprepared. In time, and with training, you will grow into the full use of the equipment God designed for you.

You've embarked upon a learning curve that ends in Heaven. Burden bearing is not something that you can take a few classes in and master. You can become skillful only as you spend time with Jesus, doing what He does. You must not abandon the learning process when you see yourself bearing burdens wrongly as often as rightly. As with any new skill, you will feel awkward at first—accuracy comes with practice. You must come to peace with the humility of learning and take on the attitude of an apprentice. You will always encounter something new and never become so astute that you cannot be tripped or caught unaware in burden bearing.

Professional athletes make sport a way of living, be it football, basketball, soccer, golf, or cycling, and they will be coached for their entire professional life. Although you can hardly call burden bearing a sport, Jesus is surely your trainer, your coach, your rabbi, your teacher, and your mentor.

In the following chapters, you will look at major areas of learning that are essential if you, as a burden bearer, are to live a healthy, joy-filled life. There will be a sharp learning curve as you attempt to walk in your healing, learn to recognize and use Kingdom language, and learn to conduct yourself as a son or daughter of the King.

Let's look at the way you learn so that you will not put unreasonable expectations upon yourself. Not everyone learns the same way. You cannot expect your process or learning program to look the same as anyone else's; neither can you expect to progress at the same rate.

How You Learn

You must become a student of yourself, not a navel gazer, but a student. First, take note of your predominant learning mode and look for God to speak, call you to bear burdens, and teach you through it. Although this is a good place to begin to look for God to speak and interact, do not be surprised when He does not limit Himself to your limitations or preferences!

If you learn best through hearing, you may find it easier to be attentive to Scripture when it is read (live or recorded) than when reading Scripture for yourself. The Lord often gives auditory learners wise thoughts directly into the mind without the usual thought process you go through to come come to a conclusion. You realize the wisdom did not originate with you, but that God "downloaded it!" He may also cause others to speak directly into your life.

Others learn visually. When you read Scripture, the Lord may help you picture the Bible scenes or see how to apply the biblical principles to areas of your life. You may see visions (pictures) as you go about your life or receive insight from dreams. Visual people may also pay attention to what others "see," spiritually speaking.

Some learn through the kinesthetic mode, in which you learn by doing. Imagine a teacher putting her hand over a child's hand to teach writing. She is helping her student experience how the muscles move and feel when writing. The wise teacher, when working with someone who learns best by doing, will not only tell her student *what* to do (hearing) or give her student *pictures* (seeing), but will provide experiences of the task (doing) before holding the student accountable for the lesson. Through the experience the student can then make the associations from feeling to hearing and seeing. Without experience, hearing can be noise and visuals can be confusing.

Researchers have identified many other learning styles; some are variations on these themes. I chose these to illustrate the point that, in your own unique way, you learn to hear God call you to bear burdens, instruct you in how to pray, and indicate whether or not you should do anything in addition to prayer. Therefore, you cannot measure yourself by anyone else. Your learning experiences will fit you, not someone else, although the core lesson may be the same.

It is relatively easy to identify your learning style. Think about the Christmas gifts that children receive from time to time in which the box says, "Some assembly required." Auditory learners lay all the pieces out on the floor and then hand the directions to someone else. "OK, now tell me what comes next." A visual learner lays everything out according to the diagrams and methodically reads, studies, and assembles. The kinesthetic learner may lay everything out as diagrammed, but then throw the directions and the packing off in the corner, look at the picture of the finished product, carefully manipulate the pieces, and before you know it, the assembly is complete. They assemble it "by feel."

My experience is that God meets you where you are and leads you into places you've never dreamed of! He will begin with what comes easily to you and then expand your repertoire of ways to hear, encounter, and respond to Him. As you begin to join Jesus in His ministry of reconciliation, look for Him to begin teaching you to hear His voice by means of your dominant learning style. If you learn visually, I would expect Scriptures to "leap to life," or you may observe an interchange between two people with new eyes as you experience the data stream of information around you. You will "see" what is on God's heart.

The same would be true for those whose predominant learning style is auditory. I would expect you to "hear" burdens on God's heart as you converse with people, overhear conversations, or read Scripture aloud. Some recognize God speaking to them through something as mundane as the television—what is said literally grabs their attention, and they have come to recognize that God is saying something and they must listen closely. Kinesthetic learners could expect God to use their sense of things being "right, or "fitting"; they will feel "something is amiss or afoot, all systems alert!" Once the Lord has your attention, He can proceed with whatever it is He wants to show you or direct you to do.

THE NEED FOR TRAINING

Training is different from learning. Learning is with the mind and involves principles and concepts, but training involves habitual responses. This is the hard part, for you have spent "X" number of years responding to incoming sensory data without understanding what you were experiencing. Now that you understand what the sensory data is for and about, you need to eliminate some responses (such as assuming that all you feel originates with you), and develop others more in line with the Lord's purposes (such as turning to Jesus and asking for clarification). Training brings learning to the reflex level, which is where you want it to be—body, soul (mind, will, and emotions), and spirit working together. Disunity or lack of coordination between spirit, body, and soul causes problems. You want to become integrated, so coordinated so that you are not tripped up or tempted by a burden, stumble and fall with it, or become crushed by it on your way to the cross.

This gives you yet another reason for having a cluster of trusted friends who can give you feedback—an accountability group. Runners invite others to study their movements to eliminate little habits that slow them down. Being able to confer with other burden bearers will shorten the frustrating parts of your learning curve and remove some of the power from the thought that "I'm never going to get it!" Others on the same journey can help you with perspective when you think burdens will come and you will never recognize them in the moment. They can share their war stories so you can know you are not alone when you despair that you will never develop the reflex to pray! You feel that burdens will always accumulate and you will always live under this awful cloud...aaaaagh! They can point out when you are catastrophising, listening to and believing the rude Philistines again (as David caught the Israelites doing).

Implicit in the word *learn* is the fact that 1) you will not always do it right, and 2) you must practice before achieving mastery. Jesus said,

> *Come unto Me, all you who are weary and burdened, and I will give you rest. Take My yoke upon you and learn from Me, for I am gentle and humble in heart, and you will find rest for your souls. For My yoke is easy, and My burden is light* (Matthew 11:28-30).

A carpenter told me that the Greek word for *easy* is a carpentry term meaning, "custom fit." Burden bearing is the custom fit yoke (the job) the Lord designed for highly sensitive people. It does not need to be a heavy weight; it need not chafe. Indeed, it only does so when you wear it without understanding, when you rebel and fight against it, or when you measure yourself by the world's standards— by your performance.

Mark Sandford[1] helped me understand how the Lord trains. He used an analogy from the culture of Bible times of how to train an ox to work with a yoke. A young, untrained ox is fitted with a yoke, but wears it loosely so he pulls no weight. The farmer then hooks him up with an older, trained ox and fastens them to the grindstone or other equipment. The older ox does all the work. The young one is learning to walk in a circle—around and around, grinding the grain. This is an appropriate task *at this stage*. The young ox can easily do what is required of him; it is appropriate to his physical maturity and level of training. When that lesson is learned, the farmer tightens the yoke so the young ox pulls a little weight, and so on, until the workload is even. At each point along the way, the task is appropriate to the level of training. It fits. The Lord asks you to carry burdens appropriate to your training, your innate ability, your spiritual fitness, and your physical frame.

Galatians 6:5 says each is to carry his own burden, or load. The Greek word used for *load* in this verse can mean "a little package." Think of the size of the knapsack that a soldier carries versus a child's school backpack. Each is appropriate for the size of the individual and the task required. You do not know yourself as well as you need to, nor do you know your limitations. You do not have the wisdom to know what is appropriate; you need the Lord's wisdom. For years you have scooped up everything you could, trying to make pain, trouble, and confusion go away, but that is neither healthy nor appropriate. When the Lord is in charge of your burden bearing, you can learn which burdens are yours to carry and how to discharge them at the cross. He will teach you to bear burdens in a way that is appropriate for you individually. He knows "the Way" that will not cost you destructively, but will still accomplish the purposes of His Kingdom.

KINGDOM LANGUAGE, KINGDOM WAYS

In a very real way, the Fall of humankind resulted in the loss of your first language. When you embark on the endeavor of learning the discipline of burden bearing, you are in a process of language restoration. You are learning the language of the spirit. Take inspiration from the Hebrew language. When the United Nations formed the country of Israel by edict in 1948, Hebrew was, essentially, a dead language, but it was resurrected and is now a vital, living tongue. You can learn this language of burden bearing, but you need to be aware of what happens to you when you learn another language, for this too will help keep you from despair.

When you are learning another language, there are definite stages. At first, there is a joy in learning. You know you make mistakes, but that is OK because you are learning. The fact is, you do not hear most of your errors. Many of the sounds you hear in a second language have no significant meaning in your first, so your mind glosses over them as non-meaningful. For example, there is a meaningful difference between "L" and "R" in English, but that distinction is not significant in several Asian languages. Japanese learners will say "liva" instead of "river." When corrected, they say, "Yes, liva." They need ear training, going repeatedly over the sounds until the differences become meaningful. Another common error is to say "he" when the person means "she" and vice versa because in the first language there is only one personal pronoun for he *and* she; you understand gender from the context.

As you progress through the beginning phase of language learning, you begin to hear the mistakes in pronunciation and grammar. You hear them, but there is nothing you can do about it except to correct after the fact, sometimes only with coaching and feedback.

As you begin to learn to bear each other's burdens, you usually will recognize *after the fact* that you have picked up a burden or that the Lord connected you with someone. Or you may recognize that you have picked up something, but not know what or how to pray. Often in the early phase of learning, you recognize burden bearing when someone tells you that you are not yourself and suggests that you may be carrying something. Many times David came home, stood in the kitchen watching me for a while, and then asked, "Who are you carrying?" I was not aware and so did not recognize when the Lord downloaded the burden. I shifted the weight of it and kept on with my day! Only when David asked that question did I seek the Lord for what was happening.

You must not be harsh or condemning of yourself when this happens. It is no different from the language student who does not hear differences in pitch and tone because those changes were not meaningful in his first language. You have not known the significance of the changes in weight and differences in spiritual, emotional, and psychological freight. These kinds of fluctuations have been the norm for you. You have learned to automatically shift the weight and carry on. Doesn't everyone? No. Not everyone does that. You will have to come up against this repeatedly, like the student in ear training and the ox going round and round, until you begin to recognize the subtle changes when they occur. When you learn the task appropriate for your current level, the Lord can tighten the yoke and add more weight. However, if you find yourself consistently overwhelmed, it is probably old reflexes at work, not the *Lord*. You may need help in identifying how and what you need to address so you are doing the work of the spirit with the strength of the Spirit, rather than the strength of your soul.

The Lord downloaded a burden into my spirit (in the example above), but when I simply shifted the weight of it rather than praying, my body had to carry the weight of it. For me, it was like picking up a heavy knapsack and carrying it about while I continued to do my housework and teach my English classes. I had much less energy to accomplish my tasks. It cost my body. It dampened my spirits and took the edge off enjoyment. However, when I did turn to Jesus with it, He drew the burden on through me to His cross. As He directed healing and comfort to the individual for whom I prayed, it washed over me as well to restore me physically, emotionally, and spiritually! My joy returned!

The intermediate stage of learning a language is the hardest. This is the stage when the student knows all the rules, but cannot count on correct production. His pronunciation and grammar slip on him; sometimes it comes out right, and other times it does not. He can usually correct himself, but it is frustrating. Every language student I have encountered comes to a place of frustration in which he tears his hair or she dissolves in tears, declaring, "I am stupid. I will never learn this language; it's too hard!" These feelings carry a great deal of guilt. Many young college students are able to study abroad only because an entire family sacrifices to pay the expenses. The guilt and shame from thinking they have failed the family is tremendous. Even if a student musters the courage to talk with the instructor about his feelings, he often cannot receive affirmation from the teacher because he thinks, "It is your job to encourage me." Students feel instructors are paid to say those sorts of things, so they fear the encouragement may not be true.

Burden bearers struggle with these same feelings of despair, futility, guilt, and shame—Philistines within, but usually with demonic help assigned to discourage you, to keep you from stepping into your destiny.

As you begin to recognize burden bearing as it happens, you will have a time of joy much like the feelings of the beginning language student. Then, after you "learn the rules," you may forget to do cleansing prayers[2] or become lax in quiet time. You may forget to ask the Lord to hide you after a time of intercession, or perhaps you identify with someone's burden, and because it is similar to an unhealed area in you, it hooks your emotions. (I will tell you a story about how this works in a bit!) The other person's burden sits on top of your own pain, intensifying it, and you lash out at the first person to cross your path.

The Lord, or a loving friend, carefully points out what happened, and you collapse in a heap. The rude Philistines, Guilt and Shame, come waltzing in, accusing and insulting you, and have a party in your head: *How could I be so unloving as to lash out? I'm stupid; I'm never going to do it right. I hate being a burden bearer. I do not want to do it anymore. Why did God make me this way, anyway?* These feelings sprout like weeds during this phase of learning. You may know the truth in your head about who you are in Christ, and the truth about His design and purposes in your life, but that truth has only begun to take root in your heart and emotions. Sometimes you can live in the truth, and sometimes feelings overwhelm. Like the grammar structures of a second language, your hold on the truth slips. Sometimes you bear burdens in a redeemed fashion, and sometimes not.

Here is my story of how your emotions can be hooked and burdens intensify your own stuff when you forget to pray! I spent an hour on the phone—no, trying to get off the phone—with a woman who was in a very difficult situation. She felt that she had tried everything. She had called on everyone who should be her support, but they were all too busy, too involved in their own lives. No one had time for her. There was no help anywhere—not from her family, her church, the health care system, social services—she was abandoned! Where was God? David and I were the only light in her tunnel, and we were thousands of miles away! Bitterness had set in. For an hour I sat in her bitterness, hopelessness, and sense of abandonment by God, family, and friends. Why were we not there?

This call came shortly after my diagnosis of multiple sclerosis. I could hardly walk, could do very little housework, gave up driving because of the energy output, and had to accept the fact that I would be unable to return to the classroom. MS complications put 50 pounds on my body. I felt ugly, lumpy, and useless. This woman's hopelessness, bitterness, and abandonment added to mine, magnifying and intensifying my own feelings. So when David came home—late, again—I ripped strips off him! He didn't care! All he cared about was the people at work; he just abandoned me, let me sit! I couldn't drive; I couldn't do for myself, yada, yada, yada!

When I stopped to take a breath, David asked, "Who have you been talking to?" Immediately I saw what happened, and said, "Oh, I am so sorry, so, so, sorry! I forgot to pray!" Then I told him about the phone call. We prayed for that woman, but we also prayed for ourselves. David needed the wounds from all those vicious words to be healed. I needed the rawness from the acid bitterness healed. We asked the Lord to find all the places in us where any residue may have gone. We did not want any remnant to remain!

You must learn to self-edit, or self-correct without condemnation, and above all, you must persevere. When you see or hear that you have not performed "correctly" or have acted incompletely, backtrack and do what you did not do previously. At 9 P.M. you realize the Lord had called you to pray for Sister So-and-so at approximately 2 that afternoon, but you did not recognize it. Pray at 9:00 P.M.!

Consistently self-editing without condemning yourself will develop proper burden bearing reflexes as surely as the language learner who consistently self-corrects will learn his target language. You self-correct until the language structures or habits of redeemed burden bearing become strong. You self-correct until your "normal" responses are to bear burdens in a redeemed fashion.

As the language student slugs his way through the intermediate stage, he becomes more and more proficient. Just before she breaks into proficiency, she faces two important markers. The first happens when she begins to dream in the second language. The second marker occurs when she arrives at a place of such desperation that she wants to abandon the learning enterprise, pack up, and go home. This last emotional marker seems to come just before some psycho-neural-linguistic barrier is broken. If a student perseveres through this period of what feels like an assault on every level of her being, she comes into proficiency and then fluency.

Fluency can take as much as seven years of study and immersion in the target language and culture. Even when fluent, under stress, positive or negative, second language speakers can revert to first language structures. It does not mean that they have lost their fluency; it simply means they are under stress. The same happens with burden bearing. When you persevere to the point that more often than not you can come alongside someone who is overwhelmed and maintain your balance, then you have achieved some level of proficiency. You can come alongside someone who is depressed without becoming depressed yourself.

When you can bear burdens without becoming burdened (pass them on to Jesus and not drag them back from the cross), when you can recognize burdens that have the potential of activating something in you and not take responsibility for fixing it (for instance, recognize that a relationship is co-dependent and praying for the individuals, but do not try to save them from themselves), you can know that these new habits have some strength and you can be encouraged. When you can say "*No,* I will not bear a burden God has not given me" as easily as "*Yes,* Lord, I will carry the burden You give me," then you will find the Lord opening opportunities for you to grow into your destiny.

However, just like the fluent second language speaker, under stress you can be vulnerable to reverting to old responses. When that happens—*when,* not *if*—you must not condemn yourself. The voices of the rude Philistines, Condemnation, Guilt, and Shame, do not have to be entertained! Indeed, to be healthy you must remove as many Philistines as possible from your mental, emotional, and spiritual landscape! Patience is your best ally. Be encouraged to seek the Lord patiently, to learn from Him, to sense His heart, and to keep seeking Him as doggedly as that ox keeps walking and grinding the grain. As you persevere, the barriers between the Lord and you wear thin and you see and hear more clearly.

As you begin to learn to do consciously what your spirit does intuitively, you are like a blind man I read about years ago. He lost his sight at the age of three because of an illness. Doctors were able to restore his sight when he was an adult in his 50s. He was overwhelmed with the visual images; they made no sense to him. There were no associations between the images he saw and his reality. A wise doctor, hearing of his predicament, took him to the zoo and told him to close his eyes. He put the man's hands on a little statue of a gorilla so he could "see" it with his hands. His hands told his mind, "This is a gorilla." Then he opened his eyes, looked, and saw the gorilla. His mind could make the association between the visual image and the tactile "image."

The Fall of humanity caused the loss of your spiritual vision. You are now in the process of learning to make the conscious associations between spiritual meaning and the empathetic content that you absorb and to make the proper responses—turning to Jesus and asking for understanding and direction. Empathy is the language of the spirit and the emotions, and you can learn to understand this language. You learned English; you can learn to read and understand what you take in via empathy as well. You have all the equipment! By this I do not mean that you can "learn" a spiritual gift; a gift is bestowed directly by the Holy Spirit. But you can and must learn how to spot the difference between the gift of burden bearing and the reality of bearing burdens in your own flesh. And you must learn how to understand the gift. The gift of sight was not *learned* by the blind man, but he did need to learn how to *understand* that gift.

That said, let's look at some of the specifics that will help you discern when the Lord is asking you to bear a burden to the cross and when you have scooped up burdens that are not yours to carry.

ENDNOTES

1. Mark Sandford, prayer minister, teacher, national and international speaker, and co-author of *Deliverance and Inner Healing*, leads Elijah House Ministries.

2. Carol Brown, *The Mystery of Spiritual Sensitivity* (Shippensburg, PA: Destiny Image, 2008), 317.

CHAPTER 3

Learning to Discern

LEARNING TO RECOGNIZE WHEN BURDENS come is most important. How does it happen; what does it look and feel like? How can you know? The good news is that each of you has "tells" or signals that alert you that God is speaking to you—pointing to a person or situation in which He wants you to invite Him to act.

The bad news is that I cannot give you a list that will ensure 100 percent accuracy all of the time. I can share what some of my "tells" are to give you an idea of what to look for. Sometimes these signs are obvious, sometimes not. Let's look at the obvious ones first.

THE GIFTS OF THE SPIRIT

The Lord calls you to pray using the gifts of the Spirit listed in First Corinthians 12, such as knowledge, wisdom and discernment; I like to refer to discernment as "spiritual sight," whereby you see or "know" spiritual realities. What a person says in conversation, a road sign, a commercial, or an event rivets your attention. You instantly "know" that this is important, and you must find out why. Words or images pop into your mind unbidden, *accompanied by a feeling or knowing or often both!* The Holy Spirit connects you to another person or situation, and by empathy you "feel" the burden, which informs and helps you pray specifically and passionately. When my friend Colleen raised her "arthritic" hands to Heaven and asked, "God, whose hands are these?" The Lord showed her whose pain she carried to the cross through her own hands. She prayed very specifically and very passionately, for she knew exactly how it felt and what her loving Heavenly Father wanted to do! When you feel another's pain or trouble experientially, it helps you pray more wisely and be more appropriate with that individual.

A stab of pain to my heart on my way back from the teacher's lounge motivated me to check on a colleague. I found a her in an emotional puddle in her office. At lunch her husband had served divorce papers along with the chocolate mousse! She had one hour to collect herself before teaching her class of English literature. Because I felt a stab of pain to my heart, I could be more appropriate—I had a sense of what she was coping with.

LOUD THOUGHTS IN MY HEAD

I have learned to listen to very strong thoughts that have no antecedent. I frequently tell David, "Don't ask me how I know this, but...." I feel odd, like I am completely unhinged! However, when I share those thoughts that suddenly appear, they often relate to something David has been researching or asking the Lord for some insight about. We have decided that the awkwardness of it keeps me humble. Giving David the answer through his wife keeps him humble!

These loud thoughts usually have a strong sense of urgency and sometimes a wisdom that I know is not mine! They have more power and wisdom than a hunch. And yes, the Lord uses hunches to call me to pray as well. I have learned to pay attention to them, to turn what I sense into a prayer and then act accordingly. For years I would have a hunch to call or visit various individuals from our church. I would talk myself out of doing anything with, "But what do I say?" and "Why am I calling?" I could not answer my own questions so I would not act on the hunch. I must have done that one time too many because as I was in the midst of such an inner conversation, I heard God's answer in my mind, "And what makes you think it is *you* that you are listening to!" I made the call! The young mother was most appreciative! She needed to talk with a grown-up who could use words of three syllables and sentences of more than three words! Listen to your hunches; it may not be you that you are listening to!

I See the Need

It is as plain as the nose on your face. You have to be careful with this sign, because it is possible to "read" what is in another person's heart through your spirit's own empathetic ability. Scripture forbids this (see Ezek. 13:3). In itself, "reading someone" is not wrong *if* it happens through the gifts of the Spirit. Obtaining or using the information wrongly is what trips up many people, and this is where sin enters in, like when you use what you see to manipulate or control.

For example, when an individual asks you to pray for her about something, because of your sensitivity, you may "see" certain things, but the Holy Spirit has not "revealed" them to you. What you see may be strong desires of the person's heart rather than God revealing what He wants to do in and through her life. She may want God to move her in a certain direction. She may want a life partner, a certain profession, and so forth, and instead of responding to the Lord's direction, she wants God to bless her desires. She wants her will to be God's will—said another way, she may be trying to manipulate God! The desires of the heart may be so strong that they are written all over the person! You must discern how God would have you respond. Don't assume that because you see something that you are to bless it or declare prophetically that the Lord will bring it about!

Ask the Lord to set a watch on your lips (see Ps. 141:3). Seeing does not authorize you to speak. Ask the Lord what to do. Is this for intercession or ministry now, or is it for something else? If you do not hear from the Lord directly, engage the individual in conversation regarding the strong desires of her heart and what she feels God's call on her life is. This conversation may highlight a difficulty she is struggling with that the Lord wants to minister to! His desire to minister to the struggle may be why you saw what you did.

In your own walk with the Lord, ask the Holy Spirit to continually monitor the motivations of *your* heart. You and I can also have these strong desires of the heart and want God to do our will! Keep short accounts with the Lord so that you move with His Spirit and do not fall into trying to control or manipulate God or use information that He allowed you to see to control or manipulate others.

Under the Lord's direction, you will see when He wants you to intercede or bear a burden. On occasion He allows you to see what He sees and to feel His grief, but it is a moment of intimacy. It is between the two of you, and you are not to speak to anyone about it!

Ask the Lord what to do with what you see. If a weight comes with what you see and sense, if it stops you short, or if you have an internal reaction to it, the Lord probably wants you to respond in prayer. I take this route: I pray to the best of my ability without saying anything to the person, and I wait for the Lord's direction. I never share what I see, sense, or know unless there is a strong urging from the Lord to do so. Be careful to hold strong urges in check; give the Lord opportunity to intensify the urge or confirm in some other way whether you are to share what you see or sense. The spirit of the prophet is subject to the prophet.

For example, "Donna"[1] met her friend Vi at the grocery store and said, "Oh, you are pregnant!" Embarrassed, she apologized for speaking without thinking. Vi blushed and admitted that she had just come from the doctor's office, and indeed she was pregnant with a surprise baby. However, the pregnancy was only a few weeks along! She was amazed that Donna knew. "How did you know?" she asked. Donna replied, "I don't know how I knew. I just looked at you and knew!" That is high sensitivity, high empathy—"reading" a person.

If the Lord had revealed problems directly to Donna, if Donna had sensed Vi's negative emotions, or if Vi had shared that she was having troubled emotional responses to the unexpected pregnancy, and they were to pray, then it would become burden bearing. Donna would bring Vi's trouble to the Lord. If she sensed the trouble, absorbed some of the emotions, but did not pray privately or with Vi, she would wear the emotions and bear the burden in an unredeemed way. If the burden settled in her mind, she might find herself battling thoughts that she was inadequate or that life was suddenly more than she could bear. She could experience Vi's emotional state, but be confused by it and think those feelings were her own.

Just because you see or sense something in another does not mean that you speak of it or take responsibility for it. You may see needs in the lives of co-workers—they may even tell you about it! In fact, they may feel safe with you because of your sensitive nature, spill out their story, and tell you far more than you need or want to know! They may walk away feeling much better, and you stand there filled up with their pain. What do you do with that? Take the burden bearing response. Quickly turn to Jesus and ask Him to come into the person's situation and do what is in His heart to do for them. Pray vividly, telling the Lord how and where it hurts, and ask for His healing touch. That response will draw the burden through and out of you. This is what happened for my friend Colleen. She poured out her feelings to God and asked Him to minister to the woman with arthritis, and God drew it all through and out of her.

I have been the "blessed" recipient of people emotionally "unloading" on me. Sometimes I feel that I have been slimed, and sometimes I've been crushed by the enormity of their load—all I have strength to do is turn to God and say, "Lord! Help!" These were not burdens He directed me to bear—they were simply thrown my way. I need, and so I ask for Him to immediately take the excess so that I can have clarity to hear what He would have me do with the rest, if anything! Especially if this kind of thing happens in the workplace, divesting yourself quickly of such "heat seeking missile" burdens will enable you to concentrate on your own work duties.

Another way you may "see the need" is through the television. You can become filled with the tragedy you see on the evening news—but what is your response? Worry? When the news brings tears to your eyes, remember to ask God what, how, and for whom He wants you to pray and what more, if anything, He wants you to do about what you see. Seeing the need is not the problem; knowing what to do about what you see is the problem.

Here is an example of how spiritual sight can be mishandled. An older couple came to our house for a visit. They were a ministry "team"; neither was married at the time. As they stood to leave, I saw them standing there, but in a split second, I also saw and sensed that they were married. I knew in my head that they were not. The sensation was like when the eye doctor puts a lens in front of your eye. There was a warp in my vision and I "saw" and "knew"—had the sense that they were married. Then the lens was removed, and I saw the reality of two single people in front of me.

I sensed that I was to speak what I saw, but I argued with God because I thought my mind was playing tricks on me. This was "weird," and I kept it to myself. Within a few months that couple did marry. Now, I believe that the Lord showed me the spiritual reality in their hearts because He wanted me *to say something*. In their case I was to pray, yes, but also to say something and open a dialogue. Had I shared the experience with my pastor husband, he would have followed up. As life unfolded, it became clear that they would have benefited from counsel. I did not share the experience until long after because I did not believe what I saw, nor did I want to be "weird." I caused myself a weight of guilt and carried it unnecessarily for a long time.

SUDDEN MOOD CHANGES

Sudden mood changes, especially after a hug, a handshake, or conversation, can alert you to turn to the Lord. Through empathetic connection a portion of the person's trouble may transfer either in the contact or during the conversation. Suddenly you are walking in their shoes. By word of knowledge (see 1 Cor. 12:8) and by empathy you know what they feel, what they struggle with, and now you can pray to the point. These sudden transfers of mood can make you think you are crazy because natural burden bearers usually assume that if they feel something, it originated from them!

Thankfully, a good portion of burden bearing is the obvious kind and, therefore, easily discharged to the cross when you become aware and turn to Jesus. The Holy Spirit gathers up the burden in you and pulls it through, out of you, and onto the Cross. Jesus responds with love that flows over, through, and around you to the one for whom you pray. You both receive healing and assurance, love and comfort.

SOME NOT SO OBVIOUS SIGNS

You may become aware that you have an understanding or know something about someone, but have nothing concrete on which to base that understanding. When you experience burdens this way, it can be difficult to sort your own problem from what you absorb, and difficult to know how to respond. I encountered a woman once—we had not even shaken hands before I "knew" not to trust her. I did not know why; I had nothing upon which to base my distrust. When asked my opinion of her, I chose my words very carefully. I did not know why God allowed her to be part of my life, but I "knew" it would not be safe for me to be any more than an acquaintance. Did I accurately sense ambition in her? Was she a "corporate climber" who would step on you on her way up, or was there just a teensy weensy bit of jealousy on my part? This is why it is so necessary to know your own values and how you prefer to be in a given situation—I'll say more about values in Chapter 8.

CONSTANT FEAR OR WORRY

Fear and worry that you cannot leave at the cross often come from carrying burdens unaware. When you see fear and worry dogging your days and nights but do not normally obsess in this way, suspect that you picked up a burden, but were unaware of it. *Burden bearing will add to any fear or worry; it will intensify and exaggerate any unhealed area.* What was a concern becomes a worry. Worries, given time and space, grow into fears. The burden becomes entangled with your own concerns so when you leave them with Jesus, they do not stay there.

Shortly after my MS attack in 1995, both of our daughters were in situations they could not change—they were helpless! I was barely able to walk, had given up driving, and was hardly able to care for myself. I was helpless, and helpless to help them. Of course I could pray, and pray I did, but the burden would not stay at the cross. It seemed it was attached by a bungee cord! I took it to the cross; it followed me home. The worry became constant; it consumed my days. My concerns over my marriage multiplied, becoming stark specters that frightened me day and night. Would my husband leave me? Why would he want to stay? I felt all my beauty was gone—I had become an ugly lump, a burden for him. There was nothing I could do about it!

The burdens I picked up from our daughters piled on top of my own concerns for my future. The added weight made those concerns excruciatingly painful. I was an emotional basket case. Their burden, their issues of helplessness were similar to my own. I still had unhealed issues, so their burdens, being so similar, sat on mine and revealed my own need for healing. When we were finally able to separate their issues from mine, I could take their burdens to the cross, and they stayed there. I then had more capacity to receive healing, comfort, and loving assurances for myself.

In His love for you, God will let a burden sit in you long enough to reveal your own need so that you will turn and be healed. He does not want to rip the burden out of you; rather, He wants healing for both of you. Two people benefit—the person you pray for whose burden sticks like glue, and you, because the added burden reveals to you your own need for healing. When your fear or worry becomes constant, ask the Lord if, unknowingly, burdens have become entangled with your own emotions.

FEELINGS THAT COME OUT OF NOWHERE

If there is no build-up or preceding thoughts, I find that emotions usually have their origins elsewhere. An event or thought usually triggers your feelings. If you pay attention, you can track back to what triggered them. You must watch and study yourself so that you can begin to distinguish which emotions originate with you and which ones come to you either through empathy alone or through the Holy Spirit. When you realize that you have been "hit" with a feeling, take the time to listen to the Lord.

David tells the story of a time he was talking with the husband of a client. The man would ask a question, but before David could answer, he asked another. David became aware of an anger in himself that was white hot. He was able to bridle it enough to say that he needed the man to decide whether he wanted David to listen to all his questions and then answer, or if he wanted to let him finish answering one question before he posed another! One or the other—the interruptions were irritating! Thankfully, the conversation ended without an explosion!

Alone with the Lord, David grieved over his anger. He thought he had dealt with the roots of it! He traced the events back, and the Lord showed him that he had experienced the edges of the man's fear of losing his wife. The man was hiding his fear behind anger. The anger that seemed to come from "nowhere" had its source outside of David—it had *not* originated in him!

The Lord will direct you to 1) mark what you experience with prayer and go on, 2) pray out what you feel and leave it with Him, or 3) carry it as an ongoing intercession. If it is none of the above, you should 4) ask Him to wash you clean! You live in spiritual smog and need to wash off build-up. It brought me great relief to hear Mark Sandford say, "Half the craziness you feel is not your own!"

Uncharacteristic thought patterns and content that does not reflect your values are suspect. When thoughts, attitudes, and topics take you by surprise, quickly ask the Lord where they came from and how to pray about them. For example, few people would characterize me as a critical person, but I had a "critical episode" that taught me a great deal.

David and I went to hear a well-known Christian speaker. During the worship time, a young person across the aisle gyrated in tempo with the worship music. Periodically she would stop and look around to see if anyone noticed. I heard the thought, *Oh, grow up!* I immediately felt guilty, confessed silently, and asked the Lord's forgiveness and help with my "critical thoughts." Then I noticed one of the "elder" types in the front row. His hair was perfect. The crease in his pants "just so," and you could see your reflection in the shine on his shoes. I heard the thought, *Whitewashed sepulchre!* I recognized that the attitude that came with the thought was self-righteousness. I immediately bowed my head and repented. I was ashamed to think these things about people the Lord loved, and pleaded with Him to help me.

After a time I opened my eyes to read the words of the worship song—hoping to only read the words, not the people! The woman in front of me jumped up and down energetically to the music, and I heard the thought, *Christian calisthenics,* and felt an attitude of disdain toward this Christian athlete. I was beside myself with conviction and self-condemnation. Now I was doing to myself what I had done to others! The rude Philistines of self-condemnation were having a party in my head! I determined not to take my eyes off the floor for the rest of the worship time.

Then I heard in my mind and spirit the thought, *But you aren't wrong, Carol.* What? *You are not wrong; I spoke those words to you. But, what are you going to do with the information?* Then I realized that the Lord had shown me a spiritual reality, not to condemn, but to give direction for prayer. All three persons were trapped in a "form of godliness" and missing the Lord (see 2 Tim. 3:5). All three wanted love and acceptance and did what they thought would get it. "If I gyrate vigorously, if I dress immaculately, if I jump higher than others, then God, will You see me, will You love me? Will Your people see me and love me?" They were unable to sense the Lord in a way that filled their longing for love and acceptance. His compassion welled up within me, and it was easy to pray for them with compassion.

It is also possible that the Lord wanted me to pray for myself. When I had critical thoughts, I was critical of myself for having them! It could be that when the Lord said, "You are not wrong," that He was saying that I was not wrong about the performance-oriented faults in those three, nor was I wrong in seeing that I was being critical. However, He went on to ask what I was going to do with the information. Self-judgment is no less wrong than judgment of others. As well as praying for them, I needed to seek Him regarding the origin of the critical feelings within me. Why were they there? Where did I learn to be critical? Who taught me that? Who and what did I need to forgive?

A NEED FOR SOLITUDE

The Lord uses the need for solitude to remove me from the busyness of life so I can hear accurately what is on His heart. Jesus withdrew to lonely places and prayed (see Luke 4:42). Mark 1:35 and Luke 5:16 make it clear that this was a custom, not a one-time event. If Jesus needed quiet to hear, you and I should not be surprised that we will too! I have felt driven to be away from people, sometimes my own family, to listen in the quiet and think with the Lord. I dialogue with Him as with any other individual—talk, listen, think, ponder, and talk again.

However, a need for solitude can cause a great deal of false guilt. A problem with prayer and solitude is that it does not appear to be doing anything productive. This is not seen as a good thing in our production-oriented society. If you believe you always have to produce or be able to justify "down time," a web of guilt can easily catch you. You may perceive yourself as avoiding people or being lazy when in reality you are being obedient!

One of those "culture clashes" came on a "Women's Sunday"—a day in which the women led the church service. On this particular Sunday, Kingdom values took priority over social convention. I felt guilty, and my husband helped me feel that way. I should want to be in the Lord's house. I should want to be praising Him. What was this intense need to watch the grass grow? Why did I want only to stare out my living room window? My husband sighed deeply and went to church by himself. He saw that guilt was not enough to pry me away from solitude with Jesus. The Lord took me into a powerful prayer time regarding a current national issue. When the prayer was finished, I knew something had changed.

The Lord may also use the need for solitude to call you away for relationship with Him, alone. At times, you may interpret such a call to be about intercession, so you sit expectantly, waiting. Nothing comes! The Lord uses whatever signals you respond to, the ones with which you are familiar, to call you away for "hangout" time. These can be wonderful times of friendship when you come to know His heart and character, times when you learn to recognize His presence and feel His love, times when you are renewed, restored, and refreshed. When these times of intimacy come—and they do—relax and enjoy Him.

MARK IT WITH PRAYER

There are some burdens you are not built to bear. They require the kind of work that perfectly suits someone else. If you pick up such a burden, you rob your brother of his task. These types of burdens you mark with a prayer, much like a road flare, and keep going, trusting the Lord to bring the person perfectly suited for the job. Discernment of these kinds of burdens has much to do with knowing yourself, your resources, your boundaries, and your ability to hear from God.

Picture yourself driving along a two-lane mountain highway. You come upon a landslide that completely closes your lane, but there is room in the other lane to drive carefully past the obstruction. The only tools you have in your car are a teaspoon and a cell phone. Logic tells you that the most effective and efficient thing to do is use the cell phone to alert the authorities to clear the obstruction. The second logical thing to do is to set road flares to alert other drivers of the problem. Those actions are a more effective and efficient use of time and resources than trying to clear the road with a teaspoon!

Some burdens, conditions, and situations are like landslides which cannot be cleared with a teaspoon. If your physical, emotional, and spiritual resources are the teaspoon, then you have no business trying to clear the roadway. The responsible thing to do is call for a bulldozer. The Lord knows who the spiritual bulldozers are; ask Him to call one or more of them. Do you have *any* responsibility if a burden is bigger than you are? Certainly, you do! Your responsibility is to invite the Lord into the situation and to alert the human spiritual authorities of the problem when that is appropriate. The Lord sometimes waits for you to call out to Him *before* He calls in the cavalry.

The prayer is the phone call and the road flare. *Then* you ask the Lord if there is anything further for you to do. Having done that, stand back and wait. You must not assume that you are either to pass by on the other side or that you are to dive in with your spoon. The Lord knows that there may be more of that mountain coming down. If you were in there digging, you could easily be buried. Or you could exhaust yourself doing the job someone else is better qualified to do. You can exhaust your personal resources doing a good thing and be unable to do the best thing—the job for which God uniquely designed you. The "best thing" will be different for each of us.

On the other hand, if you try to pass by on the other side without prayer, you may leave others in position to have the next bit of mountain deposited on top of them! In order to protect the Body of Christ as it travels the road of life, someone needs to be alerted!

Some people can carry a great deal, and others less. The Lord does not love one more than the other. Ask the Lord to teach you your limits and strengths. OK, that is the metaphor; now what does that look like practically? Here are some examples of burdens that I have learned *not* to pick up.

WHEN NOT TO PICK UP BURDENS

The burden may not be appropriate for me. Many people I relate to have very complex life situations. I am able to pray for them from a distance as the Lord calls me to do so, but I know better than to ask for specifics. Doing so may be an invitation for them to share their trouble and may evoke a long, complex story. The damage in their lives is so great and the needs so vast that my little engine can be quickly overwhelmed. My eyes glaze over, and I am barely able to stay present to hear what they have to share! When they finally finish their story and ask me to pray, I have no energy to do so. I am not physically able to bear even hearing about their burden—it is inappropriate *for me.* The Lord may direct someone else to ask for particulars because they can know those things and not be overwhelmed. The Lord has someone else perfectly designed to carry those burdens, and if I took them on, I would rob my brother of the good works he was to do.

The burden may be too toxic. The type of spiritual content of the burden is another reason to be careful to ask the Lord if you are to do anything more than mark the problem with a prayer. The complexity of need may not overwhelm you, but the spiritual toxicity may. If someone like the man from Gaderene visits the small Bible study and accountability group that you host in your home and then returns later for prayer, is your faith and spiritual authority adequate to cast out "a legion" all by yourself?

To take on a toxic burden would be like carrying hazardous material with no protective gear. Some burdens have toxic messengers from the enemy attached to them. You have the faith to neutralize some, but others you should leave alone. I am a bantamweight fighter; it is not a good idea for me to take on a heavyweight—not a good idea! I need to hide in Jesus and ask Him to fight those battles and neutralize those foes, or from the safety of a group I can take on the burden together with others.

I may be in a spiritually fragile state. From time to time, the Lord will reveal an area in your life that needs some renovation. During these times, you may encounter someone in a similar situation who needs the same type of repair. The Lord knows how strong or weak you are and what coming into contact with this type of burden would do to you *at this time*. At another time, you may not have any difficulty at all. He knows when it is safe to exercise spiritual muscle and when doing so would not only overwhelm, but cause something to break. For this reason, He may direct you to invite *Him* to do something about the need and then ask you to maneuver around the landslide before you become a part of it! A burden that is similar to your own difficulties usually intensifies and exaggerates your own, triggers old behavior, or even interferes with what the Lord is doing in your life. It is akin to walking too soon on a broken leg. The Lord knows what you are able to bear safely and what is best to trust to Him.

DEVELOP A PERSONAL BASELINE

Become a student of yourself—become more deeply acquainted with yourself. This will take some time. You need an emotional and spiritual baseline to know what you value and how you normally act so that when you are "not yourself" it will be easier to determine whether burden bearing is involved. For example, I am not an angry person. I do not value hurting people with sarcasm or explosions. If I become angry and sarcastically hurtful or verbally abusive, I am "not myself." If I become bossy and pushy or morose and depressed, I am not myself. I do not like those qualities; I do not value them. I do value kindness, consideration, and happiness. So when I begin to feel what I do not normally feel, I ask the Lord, "Am I feeling someone else's feeling? If so, whose?"

Burden bearing can sit on top of your own anger, fear, or worry and create even more pressure so that emotional freight comes out with uncharacteristic intensity and makes burdens heavy and burdensome. When emotion erupts, is "over the top," or so heavy I feel I am about to drown, that is excessive. I know from experience that the weight of burdens exaggerates emotions I normally handle appropriately. You need to know what "normal" is for you. "Normal" for some is to be crotchety and grouchy. This may be nothing more than bad behavior. If this is you, I would encourage you to find a Christian counselor, find out why you are that way, and do something about it!

Baseline in hand, begin to monitor yourself. When you are "not yourself," suspect that you are wearing a burden as if it were your own rather than turning with it to Jesus. Note what you are doing, feeling, or thinking that is different, and as quickly as possible, do what you can to stop what is not consistent with the values you hold. Inconsistencies will give clues for how to pray or for questions to ask the Lord. Why is this happening? What is influencing me? With whom am I connected? Questions are good. God loves questions and enjoys interacting with you.

HOW TO LEARN TO RECOGNIZE BURDEN BEARING

As you begin your learning curve, *most often* you will recognize *from hindsight* that someone's trouble was sticking to you as if you were a magnet. In retrospect, you see that you absorbed some of their struggle in the normal interchange of conversation. Sometimes you realize the Lord shared a portion of what was in His heart for a person or a group. Learning to recognize that you are laboring under a burden *while* it is happening is important. Learning this makes it possible to live with the heart God gave you without it killing you.

Even if you realize after the fact that you have been laboring under a burden, pray. It is OK to feel sorry about a missed opportunity, but do not dwell there. Self-flagellation is not acceptable. Ask the Lord's forgiveness for carrying a burden inappropriately or for not carrying it when you should have. Be at peace; you are learning a spiritual language—all language learners go through a stage of self-correction in which they hear or see a mistake and then correct it.

You will go through a period of time when you have to self-edit and pray about the burden in retrospect. The Lord is God, and time is not a problem for Him. He can apply the prayers where needed, even if you pray after the fact. Yes this is a mystery, but Jesus Christ is the same yesterday, today, and forever (see Heb. 13:8). He is not constrained by our linear, chronological time. As you self-correct, you will find yourself becoming more alert and correcting more and more quickly until you bear burdens in a redeemed manner more often than an unredeemed manner. Specifically ask the Lord to show you what your signals are when He wants you to mark a burden with a prayer and move on. Ask Him how that is different from when He wants you to take a burden for a longer period of time. He is faithful to teach you what it feels or looks like when He wants you to come alongside a person and when He wants you to carry him in your heart a while.

Spend time with the Lord, journaling, if you are a person who writes. As you have different experiences, ask yourself, "How do I want to behave in this situation? What is normal for me? Do I value being the way I am or was (angry, sad, or critical)? If my behavior does not match my values, do I want to change? Does the Lord want me to change? How?" Being aware and knowing what burden bearing is about and what your values and limitations are speeds up the learning process.

One reason you have trouble knowing when you take on a burden is the very naturalness with which you do it. Like a natural athlete who does not fully realize the extent of her giftedness, you feel that what you do is what anyone would do. But no, not everyone feels and senses the way you do. Because it is so "natural," you may miss the fact that the Lord wants to do something; He wants you to turn to Him and ask what that is and what you are to do about it. Here is how the Lord sees you:

> *Then the King will say to those on His right, "Come, you who are blessed by My father; take your inheritance, prepared for you since the creation of the world. For I was hungry and you gave Me something to eat. I was thirsty, and you gave Me something to drink. I was a stranger, and you invited Me into your house. I needed clothes, and you clothed Me. I was sick and you looked after Me. I was in prison and you came to visit."*

> *Then the righteous will answer Him, "Lord, when did we see You hungry and give You food, or thirsty and give You something to drink? When did we see You a stranger and*

invite You in, or needing clothes and clothed You? When did we see You sick or in prison and go to visit You?"

Then the King will reply, "I tell you the truth, whatever you did for one of the least of those brothers of Mine, you did for Me" (Matthew 25:34-40).

Whenever you come alongside another in prayer, whenever you become the "go between" to restore relationship, whenever you utter a prayer of invitation for the Lord to do what is in His heart to do for His people, you bless the heart of God. This ministry of restoration and reconciliation is dear to His heart.

As you come into sync with another individual, the Holy Spirit makes a connection along which burdens can travel. When they come to you, they will either go to the cross via prayer, or they will stay with you to be worn as if your own. You either bear it or wear it.

You have heard the saying, "Anything worth doing is worth doing right." I change that a bit. Learning, by definition, means that you will not do a new thing correctly the first time or all the time. I say, "If something is worth doing, it is worth doing wrong…until you do it right!" You learn to do it right by doing it wrong. There will be times when you see a need and choose to respond when God does not ask you to do so. He knows the burden is bigger than you. But, like any child, you want to help! You rush ahead of Him and take on a burden or an intercession that is too big for you and hurt yourself in the process—but that is one way you learn the size of burden that is appropriate for you! None of this catches Him off guard. He allows you to learn to listen and heed His directions and to make appropriate choices. In all of this learning, in all the doing it wrong, God's Word says to ask for wisdom and He will give it to you and not find fault with you for not having it (see James 1:5).

As you embark on the journey to learn to bear burdens in a redeemed way, you step onto a learning curve that ends in Heaven. Do not despair that you will never learn. Rather, enjoy the journey!

ENDNOTE

1. Fictional names—the actual names of individuals are always changed to protect privacy. If this is your story and your name, it is purely coincidental!

Doing It Wrong

B URDEN BEARING IN YOUR OWN strength has you absorbing everything within your scope like a solar panel absorbing every ray within range. Your personal spirit attracts burdens, unable, refusing, or not knowing how to depend upon God. John Sandford[1] tells that he used to take the family camping, help set up camp, then go walking about, looking for people in need of prayer. He even tells what his family thought about that, but I will leave that for him to share! Before you feel badly about bearing burdens in your own strength rather than the Lord's, be comforted that those who have been bearing burdens for many years still have lapses and miss the fact that they have picked up a burden. Here are a few stories.

Some of my colleagues in prayer ministry shared how they "missed it" even though they know about burden bearing—and teach it! The wife, who usually slept soundly, found herself having an occasional restless night. She tossed and turned until her husband asked her to sleep in the guestroom. Once there, she fell asleep immediately. After a number of weeks it dawned on her that she must be burden bearing for her husband. The next time it happened she asked him what his day had been like. When he shared the burdens of his day, she prayed with him for God to lift and carry it for him. She prayed that his mind and heart would come to peace and rest in the Lord, that he would be able to leave those heavy things at the cross. Then she asked the Lord to be a filter between them so that his burden would not seep into her own spirit and agitate her. She fell soundly to sleep *with* her husband.

Fiona, another colleague, spent the day relating to people, absorbing bits of emotional, psychological, and spiritual freight, but did not stop for cleansing prayer. By day's end, she was tight with tension. "To do" list in hand, she flew out the door. The desire to do all the things on her list morphed into an irrational compulsion.

Her background predisposed her to perfectionism. The list became a rude Philistine, driving her. Each bit of emotional "stuff" sat on the scars of old wounds that were the source of her perfectionism. Her reaction to stress was to organize everyone and everything in her path. That is until she came home. Her husband said, "Whoa! Turn around, go back out, and talk to God about what you have all over you. *Then* come back in!" She did, and the Lord restored her. She knew about burden bearing, but it had piled up a little at a time so she did not notice. Each burden found the button labeled, "Do it all right, or something awful will happen," and wound her a little more tightly until her list was all she could see. She wore other people's burdens as her own until her husband called attention to it. Burdens sneaked up and caught her unaware.

Burden bearing caught this next couple unaware as well. Roger[1] blew up at his wife and vented a big pocket of emotional abuse.[2] Each went to a different room, giving time and space for the fallout to dissipate. Later I told the wife that she might find it interesting to look at his appointment book or client list for the day. Could it be that anger absorbed from a client, when added to his own, resulted in rage? The wife knew that they were both burden bearers. With a stunned hush in her voice, she said, "You know, every time he blows, it happens like that. He just blows—there is no build-up—he pops without warning."

In a less tense moment, he shared that he often felt he was drowning in the sadness of his clients' lives. Remembering to practice spiritual hygiene helped, but sometimes he forgot. Looking at the blow-up with burden bearing in mind, he agreed that a day's worth of burdens found a weak spot, an area of needed growth, and by sitting on top of it, intensified the struggle. He could manage his own stress, but when combined with another's emotional freight, it overloaded him and he reverted to old ways. He vented and spewed out of control, not knowing why or how to stop. He did not know how to discern the difference between someone else's burden of anger and his own.

SIGNS OF UNREDEEMED BURDEN BEARING

Lack of Courtesy

You need feedback to tell you when you are not operating with the aid of the Holy Spirit. The fact that the Lord shows you something or puts some of an individual's load into your spirit does not mean you are to broadcast it immediately. The Lord may want you to intercede from afar so He can prepare hearts and put people and circumstances in place to create conditions of ripeness. If you rush in and tell people what is going on, if you read their mail aloud, they may feel invaded. *Courtesy is the hallmark of the Kingdom of God.* The hallmark of the devil is violation. When you identify with someone on your own—and you can do that—you may lack courtesy.

The Holy Spirit makes a person's heart ready. If someone resists, when you *know* you heard something from the Lord or saw a picture for her, it is probably best to intercede from a distance. She is not ready to hear. Pray for strength of spirit so she is able to do the Lord's will. It is a good idea to write out what you believe the Lord wants you to say so you do not forget. It may be some time before a person is ready to hear. People are a curious lot, finding the urge to peer where not invited irresistible. Learn to wait for invitation. You have done your part when you pray; then if the Lord directs you to do so, share with courtesy what you sensed. How people choose to respond is their part.

Emotional Heaviness

Emotional heaviness is often a sign that you are bearing burdens in your own strength. However, if the heaviness refuses to lift with prayer, something else may be amiss. Ask the Lord to reveal what it is *in you* that needs attention. Do you have a habit of thinking, a behavior, or an attitude that is hurtful and you do not see it as the Lord does? Does He want to heal a wound? Is there a judgment that binds you, some vow to be renounced? Have you tempted someone to make judgments or wounded someone by what you said or did? Like King David, spend time quiet before the Lord so that He can examine your heart and reveal any sinful way (see Ps. 139:23-24). When you neglect your time with the Lord, you are far more apt to become spiritually malnourished, which clouds your discernment and causes you to carry things in your own strength. If you keep current with Him and stay refreshed in spirit, you can catch things sooner.

An exception is if your body chemistry is out of balance. In that case, prayer or counseling may not change the underlying cause. However, a trip to a good medical doctor has an excellent chance to help. See Ecclesiastes 3:1-14, which says that there is a time for everything—even going to see a doctor! When you return to balance, discover what spiritual and emotional factors contributed to the imbalance.

Physical Exhaustion and Tiredness

As I have said, unredeemed burden bearing (doing it in our own strength rather than with God's strength) is wearisome and difficult. You become worn out, lose motivation, and struggle with depression. Therefore, it is good to keep short accounts with the Lord. By that, I mean to practice those classic spiritual disciplines of having a daily quiet time, Bible reading, journaling, having an accountability group, and doing daily spiritual hygiene.[3] Continually ask the Lord to shine His light on you to reveal any *"anxious thought"* or *"offensive way"* (see Ps. 139:23-24).

You can know you are out of balance when your schedule cannot account for your tiredness. First, ask the Lord how you are out of balance or with whom you are connected, and pray for whoever comes to mind. If no one comes to mind, do not assume the tiredness is only yours, but pray in concentric circles. The first circle represents family and extended family; the second circle stands for friends, church family, and those you routinely pray for; the third pertains to your spouse's co-workers and those you or your spouse serve (clients, patients, customers, church family, and so forth). Here is what I do. I let my mind rest a moment on each circle and ask the Lord who in that circle He wants me to pray for *right now*. When I arrive at the right circle, I feel a need to stop and explore further to find the person in that circle needing the prayer. I pray for that person and usually the burden lifts. If it does not, I ask God to shine His light to expose what I am unaware of—something in the situation or something hidden in my own heart.

For example, one time I was asking the Lord to reveal to me who I was carrying, assuming my tiredness was due to burden bearing. He revealed that I volunteered to organize an event at church without asking Him if it was my job to do. I happily agreed to take it on—I am so good at such things! I used energy resources that God wanted me to reserve for burden bearing. When the burden bearing "assignment" came, I could not function at full capacity. I had already used much of the energy organizing the event. I unwisely chose a good thing rather than the best. I did not have the reflex of turning to God before I took on responsibility! God is much better at balancing my energy reserves and my schedule than I am!

You can also ask God to help you know clearly if He is asking you to carry a portion of someone's trouble to the cross over a period. As a test, I try to make thoughts about the person who was heavy on my mind go away. If I cannot push them out of my mind or forget them, I ask God if that means that I am to intercede or if I just can't let go. When the Lord makes it clear to me that I am to intercede, I do so. Later a phone call from the person for whom I am interceding usually confirms the need for intercession. It is always OK to ask for clarification and more information.

What I have shared here is a hit-and-miss strategy, but with time you gain ability to discern relatively quickly. When you have lived your life assuming that everything you feel comes from within, you may tend to pray first about self. Do not stop there; continue praying about others and other situations as the Lord highlights them.

For much needed emphasis, let me say it again; burden bearing in your own strength rather than in the strength of the Spirit results in a bone-grinding physical tiredness. This is different than tiredness from just being busy. It goes to the core and saps all energy. This kind of tiredness is an indication that you have absorbed emotional and spiritual freight over time but not released it to the cross. Sometimes, in your busyness or inability to believe that God would ask you to do a particular task, you brush Him off. "Nah, that's not the Lord, it is just my overactive imagination!" At times, the Lord *does* want *you* to come alongside others and carry some of their trouble to the cross so He gives you some of it. It weighs upon you, but because of an attitude or busyness, you do not quickly come to Him with it.

I am pushing at the need for spiritual disciplines again for emphasis—it is so important; allow me to repeat. A burden can attach to a habit of thought (such as a tendency to think morose thoughts), an attitude (such as being critical), or a behavior (eating addiction) that parallels or is similar to your own struggle. It can become caught on these spiritual, mental, and emotional structures. When you do not go to the Lord frequently and ask Him to show you what you have collected through the day, residue builds up like debris on a drain cover, snow on a roof, or ice on a branch. Snow can break a roof, and ice can break a tree. Too much build-up in your spirit will flatten you. When I am unusually burdened, tired, depressed, or I burst out in despair, my husband will ask me, "Are you carrying someone?" Due to busyness or lack of attention, I may not know. That is when I start through the list I mentioned earlier. I process from family to friends all the way out to national and international political and spiritual issues.

When I become lax in prayer or quiet time, my habit or reflex is to soak up anxiety, tension, fear, and depression from those around me. The magnet in me collects indiscriminately. This is spiritual and emotional debris, not necessarily burdens the Lord wants me to carry, intercede for, or bring to Him. They cloud my mind, and I forget to practice spiritual hygiene. In time, they wear me down and dull my senses even more. It is so natural for me to feel weighed down that I reprimand myself for lack of motivation or for being a slacker, and I revert to old ways. I withdraw, use anger to create adrenaline, and so forth. Before I know it, I am carrying a pile of debris that the Lord never asked me to carry.

Distraction

Some people are more easily distracted than others are, but when you become aware that you are distracted beyond "normal" and it is difficult to be present, suspect that you are wearing burdens rather than carrying them to the cross where they belong. Busyness with life distracts you from living within the values and boundaries you want to keep. You forget how it is that you prefer to be and act. Until there has been enough growth and healing, attracting burdens like pins to a magnet is the norm for natural burden bearers so you need to learn to monitor your busyness level. Burdens can come so naturally and stealthily that you do not see them as burdens. They are a little more weight to which you adjust. Until you discharge burdens at the cross, adding weight upon weight results in grinding physical exhaustion.

I am more able to keep life balanced when some people I trust inquire routinely about my workload and busyness. Attention to work and ministry details can distract from attention to relationships and spiritual details, which I value. Attention to my accountability people and a desire on my part to honor the Lord *has made these times of bone-grinding tiredness* **caused by unredeemed burden bearing** *come less frequently.* However, I am sorry to say, they do still occasionally come. The Lord does know your frame, but too often, you (and I) do not! For physical, emotional, and spiritual health, it is important to know your spiritual and physical boundaries because burden bearing affects you on all levels of your being.

Burden Bearing Affects Your Body

The effects of burden bearing on the body can be dramatic. The body reads burden bearing as a stress and does with it what it does with stress in general. If stress tends to give you ulcers, burden bearing in your own strength will also. If you tend to carry tension and stress in your back or shoulders, you will carry unredeemed burden bearing there as well. People with a genetic propensity to retain fluid will find the condition worsens when they carry a burden of intercession too long.

Physical and spiritual health affect each other. Learning to bear burdens *in the Lord* can become an effective stress management tool. When you carry a burden in the Lord, He provides the resources to accomplish the task cleanly, but if you go out ahead of Him, you will bear the full weight of that burden. Bearing burdens in the Lord is wearing the easy yoke, walking alongside the Lord while He does the heavy work (see Matt. 11:28-30). He delegated responsibility for running this world to the human race. He chooses not to take the reins back. He will not say impatiently, "Oh, here, let Me do that!" He wants you to invite Him into situations and "be" with Him while He uses His power to do the job. However, if you plunge into the job of making everything right, ultimately your body will break at its weakest genetic link. Carried unwisely or needlessly, burdens add to the weight of life bearing down upon any weakness.

I know of an individual whose out-of-control diabetes became manageable after learning to carry burdens to the Lord. Another man's horrific back pain disappeared when he gave the pain from and the burden for his mother to the Lord.

A church asked David and me to help mediate a conflict. David mediated; I interceded, giving occasional feedback as I received it from the Lord. The meetings were intense, and my feet and ankles swelled to the pinching point. By night my entire right leg had swollen to an alarming size. We did what we knew to release the people's emotional and spiritual pain. By morning, all was normal, but it swelled again the next day. The amount of distress was so huge I could not pass it on to Jesus fast enough to prevent the "backup" in my leg!

I had developed a habit of pushing tension into my legs when I learned to sing publicly. If I allowed the nervous tension to express in my legs, my voice would not crack or go off key. My knees were knocking, but my voice was fine! In this setting, the nervous tension from the people filled my body and followed the old path I had developed years ago. The pressure on my body resulted in fluid retention. When the intensity of intercession or burden bearing is great, for my body's sake I sometimes remove myself from people for a time to practice good self-care. When my spirit is working hard, I need to take care of my body.

A young man I know, Jonathan, whose parents are both prayer ministers, has juvenile onset arthritis. He and his parents saw a pattern develop as they charted each outbreak while he was away at college. The inflammation flared when the course content touched the students emotionally or spiritually and during exams. He empathized with his fellow students and carried their distress in his body. As the outbreak pattern became clear, his mother taught him about burden bearing. After that, he was able to pray for his classmates and receive relief.

When I was still new to the burden bearing learning curve, I attended an inner healing conference. As a matter of course, I prayed for the conference, the leaders, and those who attended. I never connected the prayer activity with the horrible exhaustion I felt or the sense of being raw on the inside. I found a quiet, empty hallway and propped myself up. John Sandford saw me there and grinned, "Oh, you too, huh?" I ran after him, "What do you mean, 'you too'?" He said, "You are interceding for the conference." I knew there was more to it than I understood at the time.

I now know that the Lord called several of us at that conference to share with Him in the healing work that He was doing. Not one of us was a big enough vessel to pass on the quantity of emotional and spiritual freight that people brought to the conference. By making ourselves available to the Lord, we opened the door for His healing for the people. He was able to siphon the excess off others, through us, and onto His cross so their minds could become clear enough to call on Him for their own healing. We who interceded were continually bringing a portion of the overwhelming load and calling on Him to act on behalf of others. Sharing in His sufferings is hard work. Many people received much healing from the Lord at that conference. The exhaustion said that I was doing spiritual work with physical strength; I still needed to learn to intercede *in Him*.

When working at Elijah House Ministries as Education Director, my desk was near the prayer counseling rooms. One afternoon I became nauseous. Thinking I was coming down with the flu, I excused myself and went home early. By the time I arrived at home, I felt fine—no fever or nausea; I was not ill! Embarrassing! That evening my husband told me that he had been doing deliverance in the next room. I do not know if God connected me with that client so that I could pray or if being in the proximity of the demonic made me sick. Regardless, it affected my body!

Husbands and wives often bear each other's burdens because they are one. Most often, wives bear their husbands burdens much more powerfully than the other way around simply because God created wives to be helpmates for their husbands—another mystery. It can be very relieving for wives to learn that not all that they suffer is their own!

BURDEN BEARING AFFECTS YOUR MIND

When David first began to ask me to help him with prayer ministry, I was a mess. I did not function well for a while. I filled up with the physical and emotional state of the person he was praying with. We knew it passed through me to the cross, but for some reason a residue seemed to remain in me. These reverberations had to dissipate out of my body before I could "be myself" again. After we learned to pray for the unscrambling of the functions of the body, mind, and spirit and to realign them with Christ, I was able to be involved for much longer lengths of time and only when God called me to.[4]

The alignment is that the spirit, in cooperation with the Holy Spirit, sets our direction; the mind rationalizes and justifies this direction, convincing the emotions. Once convinced, the emotions joyfully come along, throwing all the energies of the body into accomplishing the direction the Spirit has indicated as the one to take. Sin has scrambled these functions. Our minds tend to choose our direction, then rationalize and justify the decision and convince the emotions of the rightness of the decision. The spirit is pushed aside and often has little input.

In most cases when the Lord connects me with someone's emotional state, putting words to feelings is an important step in the person's healing. Many people do not have vocabulary attached to feeling. It is not that they do not have feelings; rather, they cannot identify which feelings they have. They never learned to make those associations. For whatever reason, as a child, they did not learn the word that matches the feeling. There are also times when the Lord allows a wave of emotion to flow from someone to give me direction for prayer. But until I asked the Lord to unscramble these functions, my mind had the primary function, so the emotions overwhelmed my mind and words became available only later. With my spirit having the primary role, it could feed vocabulary to my mind even when emotions were overwhelming. It was operating with the Lord's strength, not mine alone.

Burden bearing affects the mind in another way. You can feel crazy when an emotion or a physical pain settles over you, seemingly from nowhere. You can be bright and cheery one moment and five minutes later in the pits of depression or going ballistic with anger—life becomes weird. No, this is not being menopausal! It happens to men and women too young for menopause! Sometimes you will actually absorb the feelings of craziness in other people and misinterpret them as your own. This is not to say that you or the others *are* crazy, but that they and you *feel* that way. Take peace in the fact that, as Mark Sandford has said, "Half the craziness you feel is not your own!"

Some of the "information" that comes to you *seems* out of context and does not make sense. As a child, you learned to either make sense or be quiet. What you sense may still not make sense to you, but now, as an adult, you may find that when shared, it is amazing how much sense it makes to those with whom you share! Second-guessing and questioning what you receive from the Lord is an invitation to the Philistines to play mean little games in your mind and to use up energy better spent on other endeavors.

The ease with which you fall prey to this rude Philistine called "Crazy-making" is a good reason for having a small group of trusted friends. There is no substitute for unconditional acceptance. You need the assurance and confidence that you will be accepted when you are "weird." Trusted friends can lovingly tell you when you *are* being genuinely strange, but also affirm the accuracy of what you see or hear from the Lord. They will help keep you grounded and build your confidence in your hearing of the Lord and the rightness of speaking what you hear. They will help you sort it all out.

BURDEN BEARING AFFECTS YOUR SPIRIT

You can become confused and not only wear a burden as your own by feeling the other person's feelings, but also by feeling the effects of sin in their lives. You begin to feel yourself to be dirty, no good, bad, and so forth. When a burden you have picked up matches a wound that you have, or used to have, it is easy to accept and believe the lie that that is who you are. That is what happened when David felt the white-hot rage of his client's husband. He used to have a trigger temper. But he had received much healing, and it had not been a problem for years. When he felt the man's fear-rage, he assumed his own anger problem had resurfaced. David felt that he was an angry man and began to condemn himself. He had been an angry person before so it was not difficult to believe that about himself again.

In the midst of old, familiar feelings, you forget that Jesus bought you with a price and that you are a citizen of the Kingdom of Light. You forget that you wear Jesus' robes of righteousness, and instead you agree with the feeling. That opens the door to the enemy. Another rude Philistine whispers through the crack that the old problem is back. This Philistine is a fountain of self-loathing and accuses you of all manner of things that build poor self-esteem, lack of worth, and belonging. You start to feel worse and worse about yourself; your eyes are no longer on Jesus, and you fall into condemning, negative self-talk. John 3:17 says that Jesus did not come to condemn; rather He came to save through forgiveness. Not being able or willing to forgive yourself is to refuse Jesus' sacrifice; it is to stand outside the forgiveness He won for you, which sets you up as easy prey for the enemy. Not to forgive yourself is literally to choose not to use the keys of the Kingdom. You lock yourself into a spiritual prison. You sit in your cell, unable to move out into the spiritual gifts or the calling that Jesus has for you. You wonder why it is that other people are free in Jesus *while you sit there in the cell with the key in your hand!*

Another way burden bearing can affect you spiritually is when you act out the sin or sickness of an individual with whom your spirit is connected. For example, the Lord may call you to identify with a critical person as you carry their troubles to the cross in prayer. If you do not recognize when you are carrying this burden, you may lash out at loved ones and wound them or make judgments. You may have been praying for a family member to come to know the Lord, but lash out in critical judgment during a time when your spirit is filled up with a burden of criticism. If you are not aware that you have been carrying a burden and do not discharge it at the cross, you discharge it at someone you love or at a customer or boss, and then you *are* guilty of being critical!

Even when critical feelings are your own, lashing out is wrong. Later, you may feel terribly about the behavior and honestly declare: "I don't know what came over me!" When you are consciously aware of being a burden bearer, you *have* to learn humility because you do, in fact, know what comes over you! Giving and asking forgiveness becomes a way of life; you must be comfortable with that in order to remain healthy spiritually and physically and to have healthy relationships with family and friends. Recognize your sinful responses as sin, whether they come from your own "stuff" or from sinful reactions to other people's "stuff." Do not be confused and act on what is not your own. Develop the habit of checking with the Lord as to the origin of feelings.

It is especially dangerous to act on feelings originating from sources outside yourself when in prayer ministry. People share very deep, personal, and private things because their wounds are very deep, personal, and private. A level of intimacy is needed for healing to occur, as well as exposure to the Light for cleansing, healing, and forgiveness.

For some people to whom my husband has ministered, it was the first time a man had been gentle with them, had asked forgiveness, had apologized for anything, or had listened to them with respect. When David helps people relate to Jesus and receive healing from a life of emotional pain, they develop a deep bond of gratitude and love toward him. If David was not clear about what was happening, if he was not strong in his relationship with the Lord, or if our marriage was shaky, it would be easy for him to feel the love and adoration coming toward him, respond to it, and act on it. When the giver of ministry reacts as a lover by loving gratitude and appreciation coming from the one receiving ministry, such reactions hurt them both.

Likewise, when a prayer minister absorbs criticism, harshness, or a judgmental attitude from those he is praying for and acts that way toward the people being "helped," both are wounded. Wounds in ministry cut to the core of a person. They go deeper and devastate more because the prayer person sits as God's representative. To the person receiving this "ministry," it feels as though God approved of the wounding behavior.

One woman went for ministry, but in the confusion of burden bearing, the minister thought he was in love with her. They married, but after the marriage the verbal, emotional, and spiritual abuse made it abundantly clear to her that God did not orchestrate the relationship. She required years to recover from wound on top of wound. She was a casualty of unredeemed burden bearing. Walk closely with the Lord. Learn to hear His voice in your human spirit and in Scripture, and act at the direction of the Holy Spirit.

THE INFLUENCE OF PERSONALITY

A tendency toward introversion or extroversion will color what burden bearing looks like from an observer's standpoint. Burden bearing will challenge you, regardless of your personality type. The challenge to the introvert is to express deep things, things that feel very private and that carry the risk of rejection or laughter. Those who process things internally will need to process externally with an accountability group. Introverts, so comfortable with silence and solitude, are often called into relationship with noisy, hurting, uncomfortable people. She must come out of self to establish horizontal relationships and interactions with others in order to understand what is happening, to receive reality checks, to be comforted, and so on. For introverts, burden bearing can be an extrovert activity.

Burden bearing can draw extroverts away from people and activity; it can become an introverted activity for them. The challenge is to spend time alone with the Lord to hear from Him. I was readily able to recognize burden bearing in introverts because I am an introvert. I knew our youngest daughter was a burden bearer—quiet, sensitive, so I taught her about burden bearing as a child.

Because I came to assume that the introvert style was what burden bearing looked like, I missed teaching our oldest daughter until she was a young adult. She appeared to bear all the earmarks of an extrovert. I saw that she needed her personal space and time behind closed doors, but it never dawned on me that she might also be a burden bearer. When she moved away from home, she began to regale us with stories of day-to-day events in the hotel business. It became obvious that she was keenly sensitive. We now believe, and she agrees, that she is a highly social introvert! She simply expressed and applied her sensitivity in different ways.

The extrovert, so quick to action, will have to build in the discipline of waiting on the Holy Spirit. The profound silence that sometimes accompanies the Lord's presence will challenge those quick to speak. It is not easy to follow the Lord beyond the edges of your comfort zones, yet Jesus is the model. He was both introvert and extrovert. He spent time with His disciples and the crowds, then went away to have time alone with the Father to renew His spirit.

To respect your design, you may have to change your plans. You can learn new ways! Before marriage I was a classic introvert, but now I enjoy extrovert activities, mingling with new people at church functions, parties, and activities where there are more than five or six people. I have learned that I can participate in extrovert activities for about six months, but then need to be an introvert for the next six. I need time to fill up so that I can go back out into the world and give again. The academic calendar was perfect for me. I had three months of intense time with students and then a month off, another three months and another break, three months and then summer off. It was perfect! I also learned that my personality type functions best with projects that have a definite beginning and end, like a quarter or semester's worth of lessons. Although I can do administration, it becomes stressful because it is repetitive and endless. When in administration I could never say, "There, I'm finished." I could not tell needy people, "Go away. I need quiet!" Neither the burdens nor the work ever stopped.

Whether it is the kind of work or the ministry you do, as much as possible, arrange the type of work and the schedule to respect the needs of your body and your personality. Find ways to honor the Lord's design. You can give out, but then you need to fill up.

My extrovert husband schedules what he calls a "sanity week" on a quarterly basis as a spiritual discipline. He does so for physical and spiritual health. Our "extrovert" daughter operates more to capacity when she takes time to hide in her room, reading everything from devotionals to novels, Scripture, and self-improvement books. She also replenishes with music, time in nature, and long, hot baths. She draws strength and energy from solitude, beauty, and the arts. Burden bearing looks different when Meilee does it than when Michelle does it because one is more out-going and vocal than the other. Unlike Jesus, who was equally introvert and extrovert, we are predominately one or the other. Burden bearing will stretch you, whatever your penchant.

You can expect some discomfort as the Lord stretches you, rounds you out, and develops you. The word of balance is that the Lord will not stretch you to the point that He ruins His own design. If you feel you are stretched beyond your current capacity, ask your accountability group for a reality check. Who is doing the stretching or pushing! Is it the old performance orientation making you feel like the world is out of line, and "I am responsible to fix it?" Or, are the feelings that are coming up from a dysfunctional family origin and causing you to feel like disaster is coming, and "If I don't prevent the disaster, whatever happens will be my fault!" The enemy can push on such feelings and intensify them. You may feel that you are about to snap, that the Lord is asking more of you than you can bear, but He is not. Psalm 139:13-16 says that He was intimately involved as your body was being "knit together." He knows your frame. The enemy, intent on your ruin, would stretch you to breaking until you shatter. The Lord only breaks what is hindering or holding you back.

What I have shared in this chapter are ordinary signs of "wearing" burdens rather than bearing them to the cross. It is because of the very ordinariness of the experience that you often miss the Lord's call. What you may think is an individual quirk may not necessarily be.

In a better frame of mind, you want to do the good works designed for you to do from the beginning. Those "good works" are fulfilled by carrying on the work of reconciliation that Jesus started, handed off to His disciples, and handed on down to you. In a not-so-good frame of mind you may feel that this heart of yours is going to kill you—that it makes life difficult. And *that* is an understatement!

ENDNOTES

1. Co-founder of Elijah House, Inc with his wife Paula, John Sandford is the author of *The Elijah Task, Transformation of the Inner Man, Healing the Wounded Spirit, Restoring the Christian Family,* and several other books. He is a national and international speaker, teacher, and prophet.

2. Fictional name.

3. Brown, Carol, *The Mystery of Spiritual Sensitivity* (Shippensburg, PA: Destiny Image, 2008), Chapter 12.

4. Ibid.

CHAPTER 5

Hearing From God

GOD WANTS TO INCREASE YOUR desire to understand how He communicates and your faith to believe that He communicates with you. God's nature is communicative. One of His names is, in fact, "The Word" (see John 1:1). You come to know His nature—what is "like Him" to do and say—by spending time with Him. Typically this means:

- Reading the Scriptures

- Thinking and talking with Him

- Carrying on a continual internal dialogue

- Writing down what you think and what you think you hear

- Talking with people who know Him

- Taking time in nature to see His power and care

Suddenly you realize that you notice nuances you previously

discounted or dismissed. With time and discipline, you come to a place where you believe that you can and do hear God. I know of no shortcut.

Knowing how God speaks gives you more confidence to hear Him for yourself, for other people, and through other people. Knowing God speaks to *you* is essential to spiritual health and maturity in general and in particular to learning to bear burdens in a redeemed fashion. A burden bearer who knows how God speaks to people personally can act more quickly and confidently than one who is unsure. Recognizing His voice clears your head and calms your heart when you experience your own fears, wounds, judgments, or bitterness. Recognizing His voice gives you confidence to respond rightly when the Lord directs you to partner with Him through burden bearing. *God is restoring something He never took away—your ability to hear Him personally.*

HOW TO BEGIN

The practice of beginning each day by spending a few minutes meditating on one of the attributes of God will help you greatly. In this way, you may improve your ability to recognize His character. Jesus said, *"...anyone who has seen Me, has seen the Father..."* (John 14:9). You see the character of the Father (Abba) when you look at the character of Jesus. To name a few attributes of that character:

- He is protective (see Ps. 35:23; 97:10; Prov. 2:8).

- He writes your name on His hand (see Isa. 49:16).

- He looks for the lost (see Luke 15:40; 19:10).

- He gives good and perfect gifts (see James 1:17).

- He is good, loving, patient, and kind (see Exod. 34:6; Ps. 103:8).

- He comforts His people (see Isa. 49:13).

- He is consistent—He is the same yesterday, today, and tomorrow (see Heb. 13:8).

Jesus always acts like Himself; He is loving and interested. So why do you not recognize His voice? Perhaps it is because it sounds too ordinary, too much like your own. Even after Jesus told His disciples that He was the very image of the Father and like Him in every way, they did not recognize Him! They lived with Him for three years, saw miracles, yet did not recognize Him on the road to Emmaus (see Luke 24:12-14). In many respects, Jesus was ordinary and spoke with an ordinary voice. Most people probably hear God often, but do not realize to whom they are listening! The following list of questions will help you see that you do hear God's voice.

1. Are you a believer? If you answer yes, you have heard Him and responded to Him by faith. Faith comes by hearing. *"Consequently, faith comes from hearing the message, and the message is heard through the word of Christ"* (Rom. 10:17).

2. Have you read the Bible and had a verse jump out at you as if highlighted? That is the voice of God to you. Scripture is the written Word of God, whether a person believes what they read or not. Second Timothy 3:16 says, *"All scripture is God breathed..."* Read with faith, Scripture becomes a living, breathing word specific to you and for you. Romans 10:8 says, *"...'The word is*

109

*near you; it is in your mouth and in your heart,'
that is, the word of faith we are proclaiming."*

3. Have you had an experience in which you felt
the speaker was speaking directly to you? That
may be God's voice to you through another
person.

4. Have you sung a song and it moved your heart,
or conversely, have you sung a song and been
convicted that you are not in the spiritual place
of which the song speaks? That may have been
God's Spirit speaking to you.

5. Have you had an experience where you were
praying and the name or face of someone came
to mind? That may have been the Lord speaking
to you, prompting you to pray for that person.
Faithfulness to such promptings will lead to
more such calls to prayer. Prayer for each other
is one of the functions of the Body of Christ.

6. Have you ever felt convicted of sin? Christians
generally seem to understand conviction of sin.
However, Jesus said that He came to convict of
both sin *and righteousness* (see John 16:8). You
can ask Him to convict you of righteousness—
to show you what is right about yourself or
what is right about your burden bearing. Many,
raised by critical parents who did not know how
to affirm, have a mindset that God also acts
only in non-affirming ways. Every time they
go to God, they feel that it is for correction.

God does correct when needed, but He also affirms and shows you what is right with you. Jesus did this for Peter, *"Blessed are you, Simon son of Jonah, for this was not revealed to you by man, but by My Father in heaven"* (Matt.16:17). In essence, He said, "You got that right, Peter!" We all need to know what is right about us, right about what we do—He knows this and convicts us of righteousness!

THE TUG ON THE HEART

God speaks through the tug on the heart. Most believers can recall when they accepted Jesus as Savior. Salvation is evidence of "hearing His voice" in some way. The Bible says that He invited you; you may not have sought Him out, but He seeks you (see Matt. 11:28; Isa. 55:3). You felt and sensed something happening; you felt a tug at your heart and responded.

A friend of ours put it this way, "I felt a tug at my heart and wanted to respond, for the first time really respond to God. After making hundreds of mistakes in my life, I knew that I was not going to be able to 'make it' on my own. I was not doing a very good job of life, so I was ready to respond to God's tug. I do not ever remember hearing God's voice; I just responded to the feeling. But that tug was from God, as much as an audible voice is from Him."

CONSCIOUS THOUGHTS AND HUNCHES

God also speaks through your conscious thoughts and

hunches—those thoughts you have, but that you ignore and later wish you had paid attention to! Perhaps it was a thought to send a card, to double check that you have your keys, to attend a committee meeting, or to remind a spouse of an appointment—that kind of thing. A friend who had three children aged 3 and younger came to mind one day. Because I knew she was fully into the dishes-diapers-dirt syndrome, I convinced myself that she did not have time to be chatting on the phone. Besides, I did not know what to talk about! Later I learned that a chat was exactly what this friend needed to remain sane and grounded. I regretted the missed opportunity.

After ignoring these hunches, I would scold myself by saying, "When am I going to listen to myself?" When I said this one time too many, God used His "stained glass voice." I heard very loudly, in my head, "And what makes you think it is you you are listening to!" I am listening to my hunches now and acting on them as much as possible. Since I no longer assume that a prompting is just "me," my hearing of the Lord continues to grow in clarity.

When I have definite thoughts on an unfamiliar subject, I listen. When I have been puzzling over a subject and suddenly have an answer or an understanding that contains wisdom beyond me, I know it is the Lord. For example, I know very little about narcissism, but the Lord downloaded some bits that became the missing piece for a friend who was studying the subject. It amazes me that the Lord trusts me to handle His wisdom and pass it on to others!

PICTURES OR MENTAL IMAGES

Another way God speaks is through pictures or mental images. You may receive a full-blown picture or a strong impression—or sometimes only a wisp of an impression. For me, it usually comes with a sense of knowing, when I have no reason to have that knowledge. At times I know I am carrying a burden but do not know whose or what it is. I ask the Lord to help me know how to pray, and for whom, *if that is important.* His answer often comes as a strong impression, a full picture, or a wisp of a mental image.

A friend shared the following story, "One day I drove to church and arrived an hour early, having forgotten about daylight savings time. I was by myself. I drove down to the end of the road and sat, praying for a while. A current struggle in me to have faith came to the surface. As quickly as it came to mind, the Lord gave me a powerful image of Jesus on the cross. I am not a visual person. However, an image came to me startlingly strong. It was as if He was asking me, 'Do you accept that I died for you, for you, not for mankind, but for you?' I burst into tears, and spent that hour weeping at the foot of the cross. Finally, I came to a place of acceptance that Jesus died for *me*—a very humbling place. The Lord knew about the time change and had a divine appointment for me."

This woman now knows the effectiveness of burden bearing on a feeling level because she experienced Jesus bearing her burdens. She has confidence, knowing that as she brings others' burdens to the Lord, He can and does lift them.

Common Images

Jesus gives people certain scriptural images repeatedly. They are standing or kneeling at the cross, standing, kneeling, and sometimes dancing in the throne room, or walking in a garden. Some people also have images of the Lord in a cave with them, a quiet, warm cave with a storm going on outside. Church history tells of religious communities that lived in caves. Before he became king, David hid in a cave while evading King Saul who was intent upon murder (see

1 Sam. 22:1). Prophets were hidden in a cave (see 1 Kings 18:4), and Elijah was in a cave when he experienced the storm and then the still small voice of God (see 1 Kings 19).

Teresa of Avila, who lived in the sixteenth century, said, "He never takes His eyes off of you."[1] Images inform, but you must not presume—in order to pray appropriately, ask God for whom and about what the picture or image is speaking. It is also always appropriate to consult those with a reputation for accuracy in these matters!

THE LESSONS OF LIFE

God also speaks through parables of everyday events, just as He did in Bible times. Many times when things go wrong, in frustration you blame satan and forget that you have a God who is interested in every detail of your life. You may be giving credit to the wrong one! Your Father *could* be pointing to something that is "off" in your life, or He may be giving you a warning by allowing things to go wrongly, by giving you an "off" day.

> *Behold, God does all these things often times with a man, to bring back his soul from going to the pit that he may be enlightened with the light of life* (Job 33:29-30 NASB).

Orient your mind to look for it, and you will see and hear Him speaking in the details of your daily life. The King James Version of the Scripture calls this *"dark sayings"* (Ps. 78:2). Such dark speech is a riddle or parable in which meanings are not obvious. You will obtain the ears to hear and the eyes to see by wanting and seeking God and by being in the habit of asking Him what things mean.

Examples of Dark Speech

When my husband David was still pastoring a church, he had a sermon idea come to him while driving to visit some church members in the hospital. He recognized God's wisdom in the idea, and soon his thoughts were focused on how impressed people would be. He had been chewing gum and at the time he was starting to puff up with pride, he bit his tongue. He laughed aloud, realizing that God was saying, "Bite your tongue, son. I gave you that sermon to feed the people, not impress them."

Another time the Lord had been correcting David about his use of a credit card when he knew he could not pay it off at the end of the month. Debt was continuing to grow in spite of God's word of warning, "Don't be in debt." David was at a conference when he heard about a Christian book that would be just right for a friend. During the lunch break, he drove toward a Christian bookstore to buy it for our friend. He was thinking about using the credit card, rationalizing that it would be OK because it was not for himself. On the way, the instrument light came on over the battery symbol, with the words "No Charge." It did not register with David, so then the light came on over the brake symbol, "Brake," and he finally understood. The Lord was saying, "Stop!"

Once, David (my David, not King David) was avoiding God, running away in a pout. God lovingly pursued him. He began to recognize God speaking to him through television commercials! Gloria Roberts of Elijah House Canada also reported that the Lord calls for her attention through the television. When something in a show or a commercial has captivated her, she has learned to turn the television off immediately. She has learned that what she just saw was what God wanted her to see. She needs to take time to meditate to understand. God can use just about anything to call your attention, even an occasional donkey! (See the story in Numbers 22.) God is very creative as well as loving.

Another example of a "life parable" or dark speech is in the Book of Samuel. Having just rebuked King Saul, the prophet walked away. Saul did not accept the correction. He grabbed Samuel's skirt, and it tore. Samuel recognized the parable in the circumstances and said, *"The Lord has torn the Kingdom of Israel from you today and given it to one of your neighbors..."* (1 Sam. 15:27-28).

Look for God. *Expect* Him to communicate every day, all day. Look for His fingerprints on the ordinary affairs of life. If you expect Him, you will be alert to see and hear Him. However, if you do not expect Him, Jesus Himself in bodily form could walk up and talk to you and you would not recognize Him because He would be "out of context."

VISIONS AND DREAMS

In Joel 2:28-29, God says:

I will Pour out My spirit on all people. Your sons and daughters will prophesy; your old men will dream dreams; your young men will see visions. Even on My servants, both men and women, I will pour out My Spirit in those days.

Here God is talking about ordinary people, not just prophetic types. He has no gender barrier. The testimony of the Holy Spirit is for the hearts of *all* of God's children.

Dreams

Many dreams are merely a rehash of the day's events. David and

I call them "pizza dreams." In other words, we ate too much pizza and it disturbed our sleep! They are the mind's way of organizing and making sense of things. *"A dream comes when there are many cares..."* (Eccl. 5:3). Some dreams are "loud thoughts" that jolt you awake; in some the tension in the dream awakens you. Others are so vivid and real that you awaken. Some dreams can seem to be ordinary on the surface, but affect you strongly, and you find your mind going back over them repeatedly. If the meaning is not obvious, ask the Lord to clarify what He was saying.[2]

Certain dreams are common to everyone, such as chase dreams in which you are on foot or in a car. Fight dreams often give you insight when you look at who is fighting and about what. Panic dreams such as, "I'm lost," or "I forgot" a class, an appointment, to get dressed, and so forth usually reveal an area of struggle you have not yet resolved. If you look at these dreams from the framework of God speaking through dreams, then ask the Lord what are you chasing and to what outcome? Is there a positive or negative feeling to the chase or the fight? Does the Lord want you to call out for help? Did something prevent you from calling out? Are you lost to God or just off track? Have you "lost your way" in the struggles of life? What have you forgotten, spiritually speaking? Dreams are excellent journal material, especially if there is a recurring dream or recurring theme. If you are not one who writes, then call, click, write to, or visit significant people who appeared in the dream. Explore what God may be saying to you through this person, or about this person.

A Two-Layered Dream

What I mean by a two-layered dream is one that has personal implications, even though it may be about someone or something else. I had a dream about a left leg from just above the knee down to the toes. The leg was swollen with streaks of blue, pink, and white.

The ankle was the size of the knee and rolling over on itself. I awoke concerned, thinking, "Oh that has to hurt!" My next thought was, "Someone needs a massage to make the circulation start moving again!" What was God saying?

My response was to go to the Lord with questions. First from a personal angle: What is blocking me spiritually? What is blocking the flow of waste—something I do? An attitude? A habit? What am I retaining, holding onto that blocks the flow of the Holy Spirit? How, and in what ways, am I spiritually inadequate? What can I do to build a more adequate spiritual vessel? With whom should I talk about the spiritual bruising, inflammation, and infection in order to receive healing? Having addressed these questions, I asked the Lord to reveal whether these same questions, or others, should be applied to someone else (to whom?) or to our church. I used the answers as direction for intercessions.

I regularly receive a type of massage that addresses a secondary edema problem, so rather than only entertain my own ideas about the dream, I asked my therapist what the picture meant to her. She sucked her breath in quickly and said, "In the natural that is a very serious condition. It is a picture of primary edema, the result of vessels inadequate to drain the leg of lymphatic fluid, or the vessels are adequate, but not working properly. The blue color indicates bruising from the swelling, the pink, inflammation, and the white, infection from lack of movement.

This dream fuelled my effort to write *The Mystery of Spiritual Sensitivity*. The Lord helped me see that burden bearers are God's lymph system; they keep His Body cleansed if they are healthy and functioning. If burden bearers are not interceding for The Body of Christ, contamination can build up and infect His Body—it can become very sick!

Always look at a dream from a personal angle. Even if the dream is about someone else, ask the Lord what, if anything, in the dream might apply to you. Then ask how to pray about the person or subject of the dream from the burden-bearing angle as well. In the Lord's economy, He can give more than one message in a dream. The person in the dream may be a symbol of something the Lord wishes to highlight in your own life, but also in your church or community. Discovering the meaning of dreams is fascinating. But beware; with dreams, like everything else, you can obsess. Moderation is the key.

The style of dreams may vary from person to person. Dreams can range from short, quick, and vivid to long, involved, and complex. My dreams tend to be short, quick, and vivid, whether they are for intercession or personal growth. The fact that I remember any dream by morning is another indication that it has some significance. If the dream draws me back after I have prayed about the obvious, I seek feedback by sharing with someone I trust, or if the dream is about an individual, I share it with that person. David's dreams are much different—long and involved, sometimes having a number of scenes.

Visions

Visions can come day or night. For me night visions are extraordinarily powerful, vivid, and have a more profound quality than a dream. Daytime visions are easier to identify—there is no way they could be dreams—I am awake! I will have an experience, but then realize that I have been sitting in my chair in the living room. Most of us tend to shake our heads when these things happen and think we are a little crazy or that we are seeing things, so we do not tell anyone. If this is true of you, you are not crazy; you did see or experience something, and it is good to talk with someone about it. The experience happened for a reason. However, choose your confidant carefully!

Some individuals have visual experiences of doing things, going places, meeting and interacting with people and the Lord. They see in 3-D, in technicolor, and this video experience is standard procedure for them. For some others, visions are like watching a video screen or reader board in their minds. Each person is different, and your experiences with the Lord in dreams and visions reflect that.

OTHER PEOPLE

Another way that God speaks is through other people. At times, someone says something that zings its way to your heart. Something in your spirit resonates, and you *know* that what the person says is wisdom and truth straight from God that you needed to hear. Often, when God communicates to you through another person, that person is completely unaware of saying anything profound. Often the people God uses to speak to us this way do not hold the office of "prophet," but the Spirit of God in them prompted them to say what they did. The Joel passage quoted above says the Spirit will be upon all of God's children. You can expect to hear wonderful, amazingly wise things from amazing sources!

THE SCRIPTURES

God has spoken through Scriptures for centuries. As you read His Words, His letters to you, He can "highlight" a Scripture. You may say, "Hey, I've read this passage countless times, and I've never seen this before!" This kind of experience is a *rhema* word, the Scripture made alive by the Holy Spirit. Your eyes open and you "see." The Holy Spirit touches your spirit, and you comprehend in a new way that is appropriate for you at the time. Sometimes the Lord will give you an image while you're reading Scripture to help you further understand or to clarify your understanding.[3]

The Lord uses Scripture to give direction for prayer. He may lay someone on your heart and mind (you have a concern for a person and cannot help but think about him and do not know why). The Lord may bring a Scripture to mind that points to a direction for prayer as you ask Him how to pray for that individual. For example, I asked the Lord how I should pray for David during a counseling session. Two Scriptures came to mind, *"Cast all your anxiety on Him because He cares for you* (1 Pet. 5:7) and *"Come to me all you who are weary and burdened..."* (Matt. 11:28). Evidently, David would be encountering anxiety in the session, and the Lord particularly wanted to be invited into that aspect!

God uses Scripture to answer questions. If we do not understand, Scripture is very clear that we can go to Him for wisdom and understanding. *"If any of you lacks wisdom, he should ask God, who gives generously to all without finding fault, and it will be given to him"* (James 1:5). Daniel knew that it was time for the captivity of Israel to end because He was continually reading the Scripture that was available to him. That was how he knew it was time to intercede for the nation. It directed his prayer (see Dan. 9:1). King David continually turned to the Scriptures for answers: *"Give me understanding, and I will keep Your law and obey it with all my heart* (Ps. 119:34). *"The fear of the Lord is the beginning of wisdom; all who follow His precepts have good understanding..."* (Ps. 111:10).

An assistant pastor fasted and prayed for a week seeking direction regarding whether to resign his position or not. The Scripture read on Sunday morning as the text for the sermon answered his question. He did not understand the Lord's meaning immediately, but knew he had just heard God promise to answer to his question. Full understanding came the next day as he continued to spend time in prayer and the Scripture. With one Scripture, the Holy Spirit resolved his concerns. He was able to end the fast and relax.

A woman told us about a time in her life when she was struggling. On a particular Sunday morning, the pastor read from the fourth chapter of John about the woman who came to the well. Then he went on to preach the sermon. While he was reading the Scripture, she could sense the Lord's presence. She felt Him inviting her to worship Him *"in spirit and in truth"* (John 4:23). She did not remember anything else that happened in the service that morning. Afterward she went to the pastor and was about to tell him what had happened when he said, "I do not know why I read that Scripture this morning. It had nothing to do with my sermon." She replied, "Well, I don't remember your sermon, but the Scripture was great!" You can expect Scripture to either answer your questions directly or point in a direction for further questions and intercession. Scripture has great power.

> For the word of God is living and active. Sharper than any double-edged sword, it penetrates even to dividing soul and spirit, joints and marrow; it judges the thoughts and attitudes of the heart (Hebrews 4:12).

Brad, a young pastor, tells of the power of one verse. While at a youth meeting, a friend came and told him, "As I was praying before the meeting, the Lord impressed upon me Psalm 34:5 and said that it would be important tonight." Brad said, "OK," but nothing came up about that verse. They did a teaching, but nothing about that verse happened. Then they went into a time of praying for each other. Brad prayed for people, but nothing about that verse occurred. Finally, someone came and asked him to help pray for a woman who was not a Christian; the prayer ministry was going nowhere. The prayer minister said, "We have tried to lead her to the Lord, but we are making no progress. We need your help."

Brad walked into the room thinking, "What am I going to say after you have been here for an hour!" As he looked at her, he thought of that verse. He said to her, "Does Psalm 34:5 mean anything to you? Then he quoted it. *"Those who look to* [the Lord] *are radiant; their faces are never covered with shame."* She looked at him and then slumped over with her head practically to her knees and then righted herself and began to scratch. He thought, "Oh, no!" Then silently he shouted that very spiritual prayer, "Help! What am I to do, Lord?" He prayed silently some more and then he thought, "Oh, the verse! The verse had the word *shame* in it!" He prayed, "Lord, I lift away shame that may be bringing her down right now." Immediately she put her face down, and when she came up again, she was glowing. She was radiant! He asked how she felt and she said, "Wonderful!" She started to giggle and laugh. Brad prayed for her some more, and she accepted the Lord. The Lord powerfully revealed the deep sense of shame she carried through that one verse.

The down side is that you can study the Scriptures for a lifetime and never hear God. In John 5:39, Jesus said:

> *You diligently study the scriptures because you think by them you possess eternal life. These are the Scriptures that testify about Me, yet you refuse to come to Me to have life.* (John 5:39)

You must believe in the One whom God sent and come directly to Jesus for life and revelation. The Pharisees studied the Scriptures, but did not believe in the One God who was sent. Come in humility before God and ask Him to open the Scriptures to you. Whenever you read, ask Him to help you "see" and "hear."

One prayer minister related that after the man she was praying with left, she clearly heard the Lord say, "He is a workman of whom I am not ashamed." Second Timothy 2:15 reads, *"Do your best to present yourself to God as one approved,* **a workman who does not need to be ashamed,** *and who correctly handles the word of truth."* She called and told the man, "I just heard the Lord say that you are a workman of whom He is not ashamed." He needed the comfort of hearing those words at that time. He wrote it on a card and put it on his refrigerator!

This is a case where the Lord applied the heart and intent of Scripture to one man's life. It is not that God misquoted His own Scripture; He expressed the spirit of the Scripture in such a way that the man would "get the point." Although not an exact quote of the NIV, it expressed God's heart to comfort, and it aligned with Scripture. It must have that "ring" to it—that God would say something like that. We will return to this idea of aligning with Scripture later when we look at ways to test what we hear.

PHYSICAL SENSATIONS

Just as some people take in data through visual or auditory means, some take in information kinesthetically through bodily sensations. While interceding for Israel, Jeremiah lamented, *"From on high He sent fire into my bones...He has made me desolate, faint all day long"* (Lam. 1:13 NASB). I learned that one of the ways the Lord calls me to carry someone for a period of intercession is to allow me to feel that person's problem in my body. Bodily sensations are like feelings, in that they give you *some* information;

but they are *not* the sum total of truth. Verify by other means, and let this be but one source of information. I would caution anyone not to leap to conclusions concerning a bodily sensation alone. The Lord is patient and has all the time in the world. You can use some of His time to obtain confirmation from other sources.

On the other hand, prayer never hurts, so you can pray for an individual silently if you think that one may be in some trouble. Ask the Lord to direct and apply the prayer where He knows it needs to be. Then rest assured it will be put to good use. Yes, sometimes you may be concerned about an individual, pray for him or her, and then call to see if all is well. The person says all is well, and you feel silly as if you were concerned about nothing. You have no idea how many troubles the Lord takes care of for you while you remain oblivious that you were even in trouble.

The prayer of that "silly" burden bearer may be the very reason all is well, or since God's timing is not yours, He may have called the burden bearer long before the need has arisen so the person does not recognize what he describes. Another reason the person may report that all is well is that some tend to dismiss or deny their feelings. Some minimize or silence their feelings; others are so busy they quickly forget disquieting sensations, troubled thoughts, or feelings. When someone reports that all is well, he may indeed be well, or he may be dismissing, denying, minimizing, silencing, or even forgetting how badly he felt earlier that hour or day. A certain amount of "silliness" keeps you humble. The Lord uses your prayers in ways you may never know.

I find this sensory means of communication from the Lord very difficult because not every twinge or ache and pain is from burden bearing. MS is notorious for transient pains. I try to err on the side of crediting them to my condition so the Lord has become very definite and direct with me when using this signal. The Lord does not call every burden bearer to prayer by this means, but He seems to talk to me through my body more than I would like. I prefer other ways because of the possibilities for error with this one!

The Lord uses sensations with me most in relationship to people my husband ministers to and those with whom I am in frequent contact. For example, I recognize that certain types of headaches are connected to certain people. Clear evidence that I have been burden bearing is when I pray for that person and their trouble, and my headache, goes away at the very time I pray. However, if it stays, then I have to look at why I am tense.

A burden bearer with no heart trouble began to have chest pains, but in two different locations. She learned that the one spot ached as a call to pray for one person and the other spot was a signal to pray for a different person. She did not consciously take their physical pain into her body, but became aware that the discomfort was "there." She knew that both of the people associated with the chest pains also had troubles of the "heart." Jesus allows you to touch what another experiences so that you know what, and many times for whom, to pray. The physical sensation rarely lasts long, and it is rarely severe. On the occasion that the sensation is intense, the intensity seems to be an indication of the urgency of the need the Lord wants to address. However, for safety's sake, call for medical help if physical pain persists.

When you pray in response to a physical sensation, you call on the Lord to move into the individual's life to take off the overwhelming portion of whatever she is dealing with. It may be a literal physical pain, or it may be an emotional "heartache" or a "backbreaking" load. The point is that the individual is in some distress and the Lord wants to help, so He asks you to issue Him the invitation. Note the symbolism: a backache may represent a backbreaking load. Chest pain may represent an emotional heartache, and so on.

I mentioned my friend Colleen earlier. When I taught her the concept of burden bearing, the subject of physical sensations arose. I gave the admonition, *"This is about the other individual, not your personal comfort or discomfort.* When you experience someone's physical problem, it is for direction so that you can pray intelligently, specifically, and with passion and compassion. This is not primarily about the Lord lifting the pain out of you—that is a secondary issue. *Always pray for the other person, about his or her pain,* and nine times out of ten the pain you feel will lessen or go away entirely."

I am a calm, practical, laid-back sort of person with a quirky sense of humor. I can usually find the humor in just about anything, but one time I experienced a panic attack. It was a new experience, definitely not "me," and I never found anything funny about it. It has given me great compassion for those who struggle with severe anxiety. I would be forever grateful to never have another!

Fortunately, David was with me at the time. It hit in the grocery store. Suddenly the normal noise of Saturday shoppers was too much. My head felt squashed from the percussion of the voices and the loud speaker—all the sounds, and who knows what else, were amplified. Pressure and noise pounded and thumped within my head. I found it hard to breathe. I felt I had to leave the store; there were too many people, too much pressure crashing in on me. I began to say things like, "I have to get out of here! There are too many people here. I have to go. I cannot do this! It is too painful to be here. My head hurts. I have to get out!" David's eyes were wide as he heard me quoting his last counselee, verbatim. He saw me holding my head and knew that this was not like me and that I was describing her panic attacks. I was touching what she experienced.

Right there in the grocery aisle we prayed for strengthening of *her* spirit, for the Lord to grant *her* peace and calm, for restoration of hope, for the restoration of options. Then I received relief. Later I compared notes with the person for whom we prayed. At the very time I experienced the attack and we prayed, she was having a panic attack. Much to her surprise, this time she experienced relief and restoration of hope. She had tended to dismiss the attacks as her wild imagination. The Lord had me experience the panic so that I could pray for her, confirm her experience, and be a reality check for her. She realized the Lord took her panic attacks seriously enough to call me to help so she quit dismissing them. She let the Lord show her the trauma in her past that was behind the panic.

The experience affected me so strongly that it was months before I had confidence to go shopping by myself! There was a cost to the burden bearing. When I learned how validating my description was to her, how helpful, I did not mind the cost. However, it's better to learn *why* you experience these things rather than just experience them without understanding and thus have the joy of living stolen from you. Burden bearing is a very real capacity the Lord gives for the validation and restoration of His people.

Karla, a natural burden bearer, went to bed before her husband, Doug. Later, when he came to bed she had a sense of overwhelming revulsion and heard a thought as it went flying through her mind, "Dirty old man!" Those kinds of thoughts and feelings were foreign to her. She knew beyond a doubt that they did not originate within her, so she shared them with Doug immediately. The sensation of revulsion was so unsettling that the two of them talked at some length and then prayed. In prayer, Doug had the thought that she was feeling something from one of the people from his ministry. A particular couple came to mind, but he was not aware that they were having difficulties with intimacy. However, he realized that he needed to be available to them in whatever way the Lord would create. Doug and Karla began to pray at that very moment.

First, they asked the Lord to meet these people, to lift the veil from their spiritual eyes so they could see each other and themselves with the Lord's eyes of love. They asked Him to release His truth to them to bring down habitual ways or patterns of thought and belief. They asked the Lord to bring healing to the wounds that tempted them to judge, resent, and withdraw. They asked for a cleansing flow to come to them from the Lord so they could experience the joy of relationship with God and each other, clean and wholesome. Then they asked the Lord to lift out of the couple whatever residue, defilement, or deposit was ready to go. They asked the Lord to cleanse and comfort their spirits so that with clean hearts they could be open to each other and to God. By the end of the prayer, the feelings of revulsion had washed out. Karla reported that it was like standing on a beach as a big wave of dirty water hit and receded. Then a second wave came, the Lord's wave of cleansing love to remove the contamination. She experienced both the sullied feeling from burden bearing and God's cleansing love in the space of a few minutes. They were in awe of His goodness and His great care for His people.

Doug knew that this couple had previously sought marriage counseling. Their counselor had some frank discussions with them on a number of issues. After this burden bearing experience, he suspected there might be more that they needed to talk about. He knew he had to share what he and his wife experienced the night before. The next day Doug shared the experience and asked if anything like that ever happened with them. The man's wife admitted that she had similar feelings, but decided not to bring up another issue—the ones they were working on were important problems of long standing. She felt her feelings of revulsion were her problem, not their problem as a couple. She admitted that she felt her personal issues were less important than their issues as a couple. But now that the problem was exposed, they talked openly. The prayer ministry became very focused. The couple reported great relief and expressed gratitude for the burden bearing. Without it, the man's wife admitted that she would not have had the courage to put words to what troubled her.

WHY GOD SPEAKS

Abba God speaks for four reasons: 1) for salvation, 2) for encouragement and strengthening or building up, 3) to comfort, and 4) to work the nature and character of Christ into you and thus build up the Body of Christ. All these interactions grow your relationship with Him.

For Your Salvation

Jesus said that He came to seek and save that which was lost (see Luke 19:10). Luke 19:10 and John 19:30 records that He said, *"It is finished"* when He died on the cross on Calvary. That day your salvation was obtained and yet your salvation is ongoing. World War I ended on Armistice Day. Yet, for many soldiers who did not hear the news, the war was not over. Jesus secured your salvation, but you must receive it into your life. The news that the "war is over" travels slowly for many. You come to the Lord but continue to have areas in your life that do not reflect the character and nature of God. You maintain thought patterns and belief systems that need evangelizing; it rarely happens all at once. In Hebrews 3:12 Paul warns Christians, *"See to it, brothers, that none of you has a sinful, **unbelieving** heart that turns away from the living God."* Clearly Paul viewed unbelief as a state that can continue after the born-again experience.

Jesus came not only to save you. He also came to help you *"continue to work out your salvation in fear and trembling, for it is God who works in you to will and to act according to His good purpose"* (Phil. 2:12-13). Like Shrek, the ogre in the Walt Disney animation of the same title, you have layers. Salvation is worked out layer by layer, or area by area, as you are ready to receive—it is an ongoing process. Yes, He saves your spirit, that eternal part of you that will return to God, but look at Isaiah 61:1, *"...He has sent me to bind up the broken-hearted, to proclaim freedom for the captives and release from darkness for the prisoners..."* "Bind up the broken hearted" sounds like mental and emotional salvation to me! The powerful connection between mind and body is well established. Physical, emotional, or mental freedom in some form often accompanies or follows salvation. Jesus does not save just part of you, but you do have a part in how deep, how thoroughly that salvation will permeate your life.

Strengthening, Encouragement, and Comfort

First Corinthians 14:3 says, *"But everyone who prophesies speaks to men for their strengthening, encouragement, and comfort."* Since people are integrated beings, God speaking to you is a global experience. What happens in one area or level affects all others exponentially. You are stronger spiritually, physically, and mentally when you are encouraged. Comfort encourages you, which strengthens you. Physical strength is an encouragement and comfort and makes you stronger emotionally, mentally, and spiritually. Healing is an important component of strengthening your relationship with

God. Without healing, you cannot relate to Him fully and freely. Encourage one another with God's thoughts, feelings, and truth.

At the Last Supper, Jesus prayed for the disciples, *"that all of them may be one, Father, just as You are in Me and I am in You. May they also be in Us..."* (John 17:21). He calls you to have union with Him that is a one-on-one relationship. The more time you spend with Him, the more you become like Him. Speaking to and hearing from God is about your relationship with Him and developing intimacy. It is also about others and their relationship with Him.

Developing the Nature and Character of Christ

Salvation took care of the paper work, the legal aspect of becoming sons and daughters of God. You became a legitimate heir of the King when you accepted Christ as Savior; you just did not sound, act, or think very godly. In Bible times when a king chose a new bride, she spent a period receiving beauty treatments and learning the customs of the court so that she not only looked like a queen, but she acted like one as well (see Esther 2:12-14).

Your lifetime is that kind of preparation. Life's circumstances and experiences, if you respond to them positively, nip and tuck and reshape your nature and character. They remove blemishes and teach you godly conduct. You must spend time with Jesus if this is to happen. A parent spends time walking a child, talking with the child, repeating and repeating until the child acquires speech and balance. A good parent cheers the little one on, complimenting his huge accomplishment of two steps, and records them for posterity!

God continually and patiently repeats Himself and steadies you as you learn to walk, look, and sound like Him. Paul tells us to *"Be imitators of God, therefore, as dearly loved children"* (Eph. 5:1). He continually encourages and comforts so that you develop and can have a mature relationship with Him. You will walk like Him, look like Him, talk and act like Him—have His nature and character—only if you spend time with Him. Jesus prayed in John 15:1-19 that you would be able to abide in Him even as He abides in the Father. You must be able to relate fully and freely as He and the Father do. Abiding in Him, regardless of circumstances, is foremost in the working of God's nature into you.

Building Up the Body of Christ

One of the problems with being able to hear and perceive is that you can hear and perceive what is wrong with the Body of Christ. However, you are to build up, not to tear down. David and I are unable to find Scriptures that say you are to tear each other down. Paul tells us that we are to:

> *Prepare God's people for works of service, until we all reach unity in the faith and in the knowledge of the Son of God and become mature, attaining to the whole measure of the fullness of Christ* (Ephesians 4:12-13).

Always build up. When God speaks, you must remember that He wants to build up, even when He shows you where or how you are wrong. Ask Him how to use what you hear to build up His Body rather than tear it down. The health and strength of individuals directly affects the health and strength of the Church because of our corporate nature.[4]

This chapter has focused on hearing from God. You must be confident that you hear from God for yourself, as well as others, if you are to bear burdens in a way that brings glory to God and does not crush you. You must be able to hear His directives regarding when, how, and for whom to pray. You must be able to hear Him tell you which burdens you are to tend to and which to mark with a prayer and keep walking. You must be able to hear and respond to correctives in any area of your life.

TESTING WHAT YOU HEAR

Abba God said that if you call on Him, He will answer (see Jer. 33:3). How can you tell if what you hear, see, feel, sense, or perceive is your imagination or the voice of God? Your imagination is not a voice; it is your ability to see things in your inner world. That is all it is. You can fantasize, and the flesh can fuel the fantasy. God told the prophet Ezekiel *"...Say to those who prophesy out of their own imaginations...* (Ezek. 13:2). For example, you can fantasize about buying a new car; that is not necessarily God speaking. You could convince yourself that it is if you try hard enough. That is an example of your inner ability to imagine—you see that beautiful car, what it looks like. You can imagine how it would feel to be behind the wheel, and the power of that engine. You can put yourself in that picture. God has given you the ability to "see" things in your mind, but you can fantasize fuelled by the flesh.

On the other hand, God can speak into your imagination as surely as you can; that is how He gives you images. The one He gave to our friend of Jesus on the cross is a good example. The Lord used her God-given ability to see something in her mind to impart a picture of Jesus on the cross, dying, asking her if she knew He did it for her, not anyone else but her. When you hear something, the question should not be "Was that my imagination," but "Where is that coming from?" Is it coming *through* my imagination from the Holy Spirit or *from* my imagination from that unholy trinity called the world, the flesh, and the devil? Those last three come from the same place.

You begin to distinguish the difference between self and the Spirit when you learn to abide. As you abide, you learn the character and nature of Christ. You abide by spending time reading the Bible, worshipping, studying, and praying. You learn who He is, and as you do so, you gain ability to judge whether what you hear matches the character, the tenor, or tone of Jesus. You will recognize the character of Christ or the lack of it. Just as you can tell the difference between the kinds of sounds a bird, a bee, or a mosquito makes, so you will come to know what the voice of God sounds like. You know because you have spent time with Him in all the ways available to you. You will be able to recognize an impostor because the character or the tone of what you hear has a different texture to it. *"But solid food is for the mature, who by constant use have trained themselves to distinguish good from evil"* (Heb. 5:14).

What does the voice of God sound like? It generally sounds like encouragement; it is supportive and instructive, comforting and healing. *"But everyone who prophesies speaks to men for their strengthening, encouragement and comfort"* (1 Cor. 14:3). If you have always felt ugly or unholy and someone comes and says, "The Lord showed me a picture of you dancing in a forest in white robes," or "With ribbons in your hair." Does that sound like the voice of God? Would He say or do something like that? There was a lot of dancing going on in the Old Testament. Miriam led the women in dance to celebrate crossing the Red Sea and escaping from the Egyptians (see Exod 15:20). King David danced before the Lord publicly (see 2 Sam. 6:14). Other scriptures refer to people dancing in celebration and worship. However, if you have felt ugly and unworthy most of your life, it is hard to believe that God would ask you to dance for Him. It would be hard to think that your dancing would bring Him delight. But Psalm 149:4 says, "For the Lord takes **delight** in his people; he crowns the humble with salvation." When you hear something, and question whether or not it was God, test it!

THE FIVEFOLD TEST

The First Test

The first test you can apply is "Does what I am hearing align with Scripture?" Not, "Is this in Scripture?" but does this align with Scripture? Let's apply this to the "word" about dancing in the forest. There are many passages of Scripture where the Lord talks about people dancing. There is a beautiful Scripture in Zephaniah 3:17. The NIV reads, *"The Lord your God is with you, He is mighty to save. He will take great delight in you, He will quiet you with His love, He will rejoice over you with singing."* Earlier in verse 14, it reads, *"Sing, oh daughter of Zion, Shout aloud, O Israel! Be glad and rejoice with all your heart, Oh daughter of Jerusalem!"* The references earlier to Miriam dancing, King David dancing before the Lord, and people dancing in celebration and worship—here you see quieting, singing, rejoicing, and dancing. In this case, yes, the "word" aligns with Scripture.

The disciples saw tongues of fire on their heads at Pentecost (see Acts 2). Tongues of fire, for Heaven's sake! Are there places in Scripture before Acts where there were tongues of fire on people's heads? No. Peter could have said, "This is not Scriptural. We are not going to give this experience validation. This is not in Scripture, so it can't be from the Holy Spirit." If he had taken that stance, Pentecost could possibly have been squelched before it started!

However, he looked at it and asked if it aligned with Scripture. It did. The imagery of fire is definitely there. Many references in

Scripture connect fire with God; however, at Pentecost the Lord used it in a slightly different way. So the question to ask is, "Does what I hear (see or sense) align with Scripture, rather than, "Is it entirely in Scripture?" The Lord is pouring out His Spirit on all people in these days (see Joel 2:28). Isaiah 43:19 says, *"See, I am doing a **new thing!** Now it springs up; do you not perceive it? I am making a way in the desert and streams in the wasteland."* God is doing new things in ways and places where you may not expect Him. He is bringing all kinds of revelations and experiences that will stretch a hard, rigid application of Scripture. What you hear and experience has to align with the Word of God, but it might be "new" because He is doing new things.

The Second Test

The second test is to ask, "Do the things I am hearing and seeing find agreement with the spiritual discernment of my community of faith, the people I trust?" You might see a picture of yourself at the cross and Jesus dying on that cross, asking you to go to a distant country to do a short-term mission. If you were to question whether the Lord might ask you that, you could go to your pastor or others you trust and ask what they think. Was that really Jesus; would Jesus say something like that? If you trust your pastor or friend and trust that he hears from the same Holy Spirit that you do, you can trust that he will be able to give you good counsel. An accountability group could also have this function.

The Third Test

The third test is to ask, "Does what I hear bear the witness of the Holy Spirit?" By this I mean, does the Holy Spirit confirm by giving you the Lord's peace? The Lord gives you the ability to receive His peace about what He says, whereas many things people say do not give you peace. If you continue to feel something is "wrong" and cannot rest in what someone says or presents, you do not have peace. Continue to pursue the Lord to reveal the source of the lack of peace until that "witness" is there. If I cannot find the Lord's peace, I find it best to put the "word" on a shelf I have labeled "mystery." The third test is not only to see if the Holy Spirit gives you an inner peace, but if that peace continues.

A friend told us that many years ago she gave a baby up for adoption and then found the child some 20 years later. Before she found her, in those few years when she started to pray to find the child, she shared her desire with a couple of people. One of them prayed about it and said to her prophetically, "You will never see your daughter in this life." Our friend felt as if a spear went through her back. The prophetic word created a great deal of anxiety because she wanted with all her heart to find this daughter. She wondered if her desire was not from God; was she not to look for her daughter anymore? Over the course of the next year, she prayed about it with three or four people, and every time they came away feeling that the first word was not from God. The results of this negative "word" brought fear and anxiety rather than peace. She finally renounced it and asked the person praying with her to literally and figuratively take that spear out of her back. The following year she found her daughter, and they have a wonderful relationship.

The fruit of what God says to you, even if it is a conviction of sin, ultimately brings peace, not fear and anxiety. Conviction of sin can and does bring fear and anxiety; but when responded to with repentance, it ultimately brings peace. If there is no peace, you can question whether the word is from God or not. The witness of the Holy Spirit is a powerful thing. Sometimes you will need to pray with someone else to be sure, as our friend did in the story above. God's deep peace, the witness of the Holy Spirit, is a powerful thing.

The Fourth Test

The fourth test is to ask if what you hear is consistent with the character and nature of Jesus. Let's take, for example, a person who feels that "God" told her to divorce her husband without first attempting to resolve problems through marriage counseling. Would Jesus do this kind of thing if He were physically present? Matthew 5:24 says, *"Leave your gift there in front of the altar. **First go and be reconciled to your brother;** then come and offer your gift."* The principle is to resolve issues between people before worshipping God. If you have something against your "brother" or spouse, you have something against, or between you and God. I take this scripture to mean that you should get it right between the two of you so that there will be nothing to interfere with your worship of God. Matthew 19:8 says, Jesus replied, *"Moses permitted you to **divorce your wives** [spouses] because your hearts were hard. But it was not this way from the beginning."* There is a time and place for divorce, but it should always be the option of last resort, not the first. To make no effort to resolve issues between the two of them is hardly consistent with the character of Jesus who gave His life to reconcile us to God.

Would such action be consistent with Jesus' character? To me, the answer is clearly no.

The Fifth Test

The fifth test is to ask if what you hear is consistent with solid doctrine. For example, someone may say, "God told me to stop attending church because I can find God out in nature." In Hebrews 10:25 Paul admonishes, *"Let us not give up meeting together, as some are in the habit of doing, but let us encourage one another—and all the more as you see the Day approaching.*" It would be good for everyone to be solidly grounded in the historical teachings of the faith. The Nicene Creed is a concise statement of those basic doctrines. Should questions occur, your pastors are a good source.

In summary, these five questions are tests that you can apply to double-check your hearing, a guide you can depend upon.

1. Does what I hear align with Scripture?

2. Does it find agreement with the discernment of Christians I trust?

3. Does it witness and continue to witness to me through the Holy Spirit?

4. Is it consistent with the nature and character of Christ?

5. Is it consistent with historic Church doctrine?

All tests of your hearing depend upon continually abiding in Jesus. You constantly renew your mind by reading the Scriptures and by having individual and corporate worship and prayer. Unless you abide and renew your mind, you will not learn the nature and character of God and will be vulnerable to being tossed about by various words you hear (see Eph. 4:11-16). Take the time to seek the Lord for direction with these guidelines in mind.

Ask the Lord questions; He likes to answer them; He is a good teacher. The Holy Spirit is the one who brings truth, and some of that truth comes when you ask questions. David and I have come to a place where we ask the Lord many questions. We do not always have to wait for revelation; indeed, revelation sometimes comes because we ask questions. We wait, worship, read, and listen, but we also ask questions.[5]

The Lord is awakening our ears (the whole Church) to hear His voice. Isaiah 50:4-5 says,

> *The Sovereign Lord has given Me an instructed tongue to know the word that sustains the weary. He wakens Me morning by morning, wakens My ear to listen like one being taught. The Sovereign Lord has opened My ears, and I have not been rebellious; I have not drawn back.*

Jesus our Shepherd said, *"My sheep listen to My voice..."* (John 10:27). The bottom line for Christians (especially burden bearers) is this, "Do you believe what Jesus said in John 10:27 or not?" Do you really believe that when Jesus said, *"My sheep listen to My voice,"* He meant you? Or was He just saying that only the "spiritual people" will hear His voice? He did not say, "If you fast you will hear it" or "if you are lucky...!" He simply said, *"My sheep listen to My voice."* Are you a sheep?

You will grow in confidence that you hear His directions regarding prayer (who, what, where, when, and for how long) as your confidence grows that you can and do hear the voice of God. The physical and spiritual well-being of every burden bearer reflects this confidence. You are more likely to respond with prayer and bear burdens in a redeemed fashion when you have a sense of direction as to how to pray about a burden.

Burden bearing is not a rigid way of life. You do not have to "walk the line" as Johnny Cash used to sing. God is not going to disown you if you do not *do it right!* The individual or situation He calls you to intercede for is not going to implode if you make mistakes. Yes, you are important, and the part you play is important, but the universe does not rest on your shoulders. Isaiah 9:6 says, *"...The government will be on His* [Jesus'] *shoulders...,"* not yours! Mistakes will make a difference, but nothing catches God by surprise. He always has a backup.

Burden bearing is one of the key ways the Lord works the character and nature of Jesus into His sons and daughters. Taking on Jesus' character and nature cannot happen only at the mind level; it has to happen at the heart level, and it happens much more quickly and easily when you are confident that you hear Him.

Now let us look at some of the things that block hearing God.

ENDNOTES

1. Teresa of Avila, *The Way of Perfection* (London:Baker), 1919 p. 81 .

2. John Paul Jackson's Dream Journal and tape series on dreams is an excellent resource. www.streamsministries.com.

3. Word studies are an alternative way of spending time in Scripture. Examples can be found at the following site: thequickenedword.com or write to Paul & Gretel Haglin, Resurrection Christian Ministries, 300 Eagles Nest Farm Road, Hawk Point, MO 63349, FAX 636-597-3743. Their newsletters are often based on word studies.

4. Carol Brown, *The Mystery of Spiritual Sensitivity* (Shippensburg, PA: Destiny Image, 2008), 23-46, 115-117 for the discussion or our corporate nature.

5. For an additional resource on this subject, see Mark and Patti Virkler, *Dialogue with God* (Gainesville, FL: Bridge-Logos, 1998).

CHAPTER 6

Blocks to Hearing

WHEN GOD DOES NOT RESPOND

YOU ASK GOD QUESTIONS ABOUT the burden you sense, but He does not seem to answer in any way you recognize. You know you are to bring something to the cross. You feel the weight of it in your spirit, but again, have no clue about who, what, or why. At other times you ask for direction for your life, directions for prayer for your friends and family, your community, and the world at large; the silence is deafening. You tend to become discouraged and feel that you cannot hear from God. Your head tells you that God speaks, but you cannot seem to hear. The reasons for hearing difficulties discussed in this chapter apply to all Christians, not just burden bearers. But because of the way burden bearers are wired, the silence or apparent lack of response is especially painful.

You May Not Be Asking the Right Questions

My husband has experienced not receiving an answer to his questions during prayer ministry! That's not the time you want the Lord to be silent. Rather than give up, he has asked a different question, approached from a different angle, and then heard the Lord's response. At other times he heard an answer to his first question, but it seemed like a strange response, as if the Lord gave him the answer to the question he should have asked! Keeping to the subject, but going back and approaching it differently often yielded an answer.

I am not suggesting that the Lord will toy with you, requiring you to "say it right," or that He will dangle answers to your dilemma like yarn in front of a kitten. You may have part of the picture and ask questions based on that part, but it may not be a *strategic* part. God is a loving Father. He will endure your impatience with His silence, but will not deprive you of the learning and strengthening that happens as you press Him for answers. He knows that the struggle will bring you into more and more contact with Him who is the Answer—the struggle involves relationship, which you need.

You Do Not or Cannot Understand the Answer

If God did answer all your questions—about who, what, where, when, why, and how—it is possible that you would not understand. God is your Father; like every good parent, He will not give an adult explanation to a young child. Jesus said to His disciples, *"I have many more things to say to you, but you cannot bear them now"* (John 16:12 NASB). The disciples did not yet have the inner structures and inner strength to bear the weight of those spiritual realities. You and I are not so different! In addition, you would not understand many things even if He told you! Spiritual realities exist that the human mind was not designed to understand. It is humbling to acknowledge that your capacity for understanding, reason, and logic is not vast enough to comprehend God and His ways.

YOU DO NOT KNOW WHAT TO ASK FOR

Romans 8:26-27 says,

>*...We do not know what we ought to pray for, but the Spirit Himself intercedes for us with groans that words cannot express. And He who searches our hearts knows the mind of the Spirit, because the Spirit intercedes for the saints in accordance with God's will.*

Not knowing particulars about the burden God places in you, but praying anyway, is an exercise in humble obedience, something you need to practice regularly! Praying in the spirit is a prayer of trust because you do not know how the Spirit will translate your prayer. It is an expression of trust in God's good plans for you and for those for whom you pray. It is a prayer that gives Him control, and it is an opportunity for you to practice the servant role.

Job is a good example of a man full of questions—only once did God answer to the point! If God had given him specific explanations to the questions he asked, Job's eyes would have glazed over, and he would not have understood much, if anything. After the Lord's long dissertation on things Job did not ask, Job admitted, *"...Surely I spoke of things I did not understand, things too wonderful for me to know"* (Job 42:3). In other words, he said, "Sorry, God for shooting off my mouth. I didn't know what I was talking about." However, the Lord *met* Job. Meeting God was what Job really needed—it gave him a new perspective and the emotional assurance that God cared. All Christians need those two things, but especially highly sensitive burden bearers.

IT IS NOT TIME FOR YOU TO KNOW

God may not give you the answers to your questions because something is not yet ready. If you need an answer "right now," you may hear "wait!" Who wants to wait? If the Lord gave the answers when you asked, you might strive to make things happen—you can hurt others and yourself by trying too hard. The Lord always wants "the most bang for His buck" so He waits for the "optimum" time. Scripture uses the phrase, "in the fullness of time" to describe this waiting. *"When the fullness of the time came, God sent His son"* (Gal. 4:4 NASB). If this was true of His coming, He will certainly wait for "the fullness of time" in which to answer your prayers. When everything is right, God acts. He works to bring people and circumstances together for a sovereign encounter; suddenly you receive answers. Your questions may be good questions, appropriate questions, but the time for answers has not arrived.

THE LORD WANTS YOUR OBEDIENCE

Development of an obedient heart may be God's purpose rather than providing you with particular knowledge and understanding. The Lord always wants obedient prayers inviting Him to do what is on His heart to do for His people. If the burden lifts after you pray in the spirit, your job is done. Your unbelief and striving (trying too hard to do what is not yours to do) interfere with His work. You may argue with Him from time to time about what He wants to do and try to tell Him how to do His job. This is not good for you so He simply does not respond. He knows you well! Sometimes the Lord wants you to pray in a very general direction, such as "Lord, I bless whatever You are doing" or "Lord, I invite You to do what is in Your heart to do for Your people. Come Lord Jesus." This is an invitation for Him to roll up His sleeves and work on your behalf without your knowing specifics.

Some Things Are None of Your Business

Jesus' response to the disciples' question regarding end-time events was that even He did not know (see Matt. 24:36). People are curious creatures and do not always know when to stop questioning. Peter asked Jesus for more information about how John would die, and Jesus' answer was, *"What is that to you?"* (John 21:20-22). In today's parlance He would probably say, "Peter, the other guy's destiny is between him and Me; that is none of your business."

You may be especially tempted to ask for too many details when you know you bear a burden for someone you know. The Lord's silence may suggest that you are not to ask. He respects each person and knows that some situations call for more privacy than others do. You can be confident that the Lord will give you answers to appropriate questions. I do not believe Peter was malicious at all in the above passage; he simply did not know what was an appropriate boundary in that situation. As part of the learning curve, you will also ask some inappropriate questions. *Please* do not rush to condemn yourself. You will learn how to discern what is appropriate to ask. Appropriateness will differ from situation to situation.

Lord, keep me from being curious about things that are not mine to know. Help me be patient to wait on You for your answers and not be discouraged with Your timeline. Keep me humble so that I do not interject myself in people's lives in the guise of "needing" details of their situation in order to pray for them. On the other hand, help me to hear You clearly when I am to be bold to pursue—not for curiosity, but for what You want to do in a person's life. Father, I want to respect people the way You do.

OUTSIDE INTERFERENCE

Times of no response are sometimes thick with confusion or oppression, requiring that you pray in the spirit for a time to "clear the air." This is true if you are seeking answers regarding burdens or answers for yourself. After prayer, you will more likely be able to hear from God. It took an angel 21 days to penetrate the "outside interference" to deliver God's message to Daniel (see Dan. 10:13). The Lord wants you to call on Him to be your Champion, to fight *in your place,* when the enemy picks a fight with you or harasses you. You have the right and the authority to ask the Lord and His heavenly hosts to fight in your place. Your most powerful fighting posture is one of prayer. In those times, your trust and faith will grow as you watch Him remove the blocks of the enemy.

Another time to suspect enemy interference is when you seek to hear from the Lord or sense His presence, but all you sense and see is blackness, confusion, or blankness—nothing happening. You may be bumping into a demonic block meant to erode your hope and trust. As you try to walk in faith, you encounter times when *it feels as though* your faith is jerked out from under you.

However, it is not faith that is jerked out; rather, the powers of darkness gleefully pummel your hope and trust. Hope, trust, and faith intertwine. Standing in faith is difficult when your trust and hope are battered.

Galatians 2:20 says, *"...I no longer live, but Christ lives in me,"* and then it goes on to say, *"So I live my life in this earthly body by **trusting** in the Son of God who loves me and gave Himself for me."* Many quote that verse, *"I have been crucified with Christ, I myself no longer live, but Christ lives in me..."* and then stop, but the Scripture goes on. It says, *"So, I live my life in this earthly body by **trusting** in the Son of God...."* Trusting is the essence of faith. You cannot really have faith without trust. Christian faith is not merely believing in a system of values or religious ideas; it is *trusting* in the Son of God. You cannot live in trust if you do not know who the Son of God is, if you are full of judgments that say that He cannot help, that He is powerless, or that you do not need Him. You can have faith that a chair will hold you. You trust that chair when you sit on it. Trust puts the faith to action.

"Faith comes from hearing..." (Rom. 10:17 NASB). You have to be able to hear the Lord through any or all of the ways we talked about in the last chapter: through the Scriptures, other people, the events of your life, dreams, an inner prompting, or the witness of the Holy Spirit. You have to hear Him in some way in order to have faith. Otherwise, you are blind and unable to walk in trust.

Once you have walked through a difficult situation or circumstance and have an inner witness, then you are usually in a place where nothing can take away from you the faith and trust in Him that you have learned through that time. I say "usually" because you never know what sort of thing is going to happen with people's lives or what they are going to choose to do by their free will. *Usually* you can stand solidly in the place of faith after you have walked through a difficult situation in which the Lord has proven Himself to you.

Another type of demonic block is to hear from a false Jesus. This is something you need not to be afraid of, but need to know about. When you know the character of Jesus, then you are able to tell the difference or have someone pray with you to help you tell the difference. For instance, someone may see, hear, or sense Jesus, but instead of being a shepherd with a staff, He appears as a shepherdess with a staff. You can say, *"Lord Jesus, I renounce any false image of you. Would You reveal the truth to me about who You are?"* Usually a false image will fall away, but that is not the end of it. You need to know why you were vulnerable to seeing such a false image. These images usually attach to something you *believe,* something that Jesus wants you to see. You may believe something about Him that distorts and results in a false image. The Lord wants to uncover it so you can repent and receive the truth about His character.

A woman related that a number of years ago she was praying about her desire to come much closer to the Lord and asked Him to meet with her. She saw an image of the Lord and was meditating on that and worshipping Him. Suddenly it became sexual, and she thought, "Oh, oh, what is this! What *is* this?" She renounced it and asked where it came from. The Lord showed her that historically when she had any kind of friendship with a man, at some point he would want sex. She made a judgment that all men will eventually want sex, and Jesus is a man, so obviously He is the same. God wanted to break that, so it was good that the Lord allowed her to see that false image.

Usually a person tries to either block it out or run away; instead, you need to ask Him why you see what you see, where it came from, and what you believe that would allow you to see Him that way. Usually it is something simple. He does not want you to see Him in any way other than truthfully. This woman had to realize that for her, past experiences laminated sexuality to intimacy. God needed to separate them before she could continue to grow in intimacy with Him. It was important that she not simply try to block it out or run away from the false image.

Men may find that the image of God has something fearful attached because of the way a woman caused them hurt. She may have criticized or judged, and he believed that God would do the same. It boils down to this question, "What is your picture of intimacy?" As you clear your picture of intimacy of distortions and pollutions from the world, your relationship with Jesus will grow.

 Lord Jesus, I ask You to take up my cause. Where the enemy pummels my hope and trust, I ask You to come to my aid. Show me what the enemy considers his legal right to harass me. I repent of what gave the enemy this legal ground and ask You to build my faith. Remove the distortion of my picture of intimacy with you, and show me what true intimacy really looks like. I want to receive the truth, Lord.

A type of outside interference that you have some control over is your physical environment. Jesus withdrew to a quiet place to spend time with the Father. It is difficult to hear God if your environment is distracting. You need a sanctum sanctorum, a Holy of Holies, where you can go to hide away with God. If you do not have one already, do your best to create one!

INTERNAL INTERFERENCE

When you accepted Jesus as Lord and Savior, He adopted you into His family; you became a son or daughter of God. If you have trouble believing in God's goodness, now would be a good time to suck in your breath and "choose to believe" that God is good. Your feelings may tell you otherwise, but feelings are transient; they pass. They reflect your state of being at the moment; they do not reflect eternal, enduring truth. If you have spent time immersed in Scripture, prayer, worship, and journaling, you will have a better sense of the nature and character of Christ. It will be easier to follow whatever directions you have, even in the presence of apparent silence on His part.

It is also possible that the silence you hear and sense is not silence on God's part. The most common reason a person is unable to hear God's voice is that there is a block or blocks in your human spirit that prevent you from hearing. You may perceive it to be His silence when, in fact, the difficulty is yours. The rest of this chapter deals with some of the most common of these blocks.

MENTAL BLOCK

Dreams, pictures, and visions are easy to see when you are not trying to. When you are asleep or "spaced out," the Lord can bypass the interference of the mind. When you were a child, you did something or something happened to you that embarrassed or humiliated you. You determined (subconsciously, of course) never to allow that to happen again so you assigned your mind the task of making sure you did not do "something stupid" ever again. In so doing, you gave the mind the role of monitoring and guarding. "You are to say and do nothing without first passing mental tests, 'Is this logical?' 'Is it socially acceptable?' and so forth." You depend upon your mind to keep you safe and help you figure out life. You put the mind in the director's chair, but the Lord's order is that the spirit is to set the direction for your life based upon the Word of God: *"It is the spirit in a man, the breath of the Almighty, that gives him understanding"* (Job 32:8). Society, science, and technology relegated the spirit to a minor role and elevated the mind for what *you believed at the time* to be safety reasons. You can develop your mind so much that you leave your human spirit pining in the back room. Not only do you depend upon your mind to keep you safe, but also to discard whatever it perceives to be unimportant. Many people hear from the Lord, but discard it, thinking automatically that whatever is in the mind is "just me, just my imagination"; they do not recognize the Lord's voice.

 Lord Jesus, to the extent that I have put my mind in charge of my life and have depended upon it to keep me safe, to understand everything, and to filter out "meaningless" data, I ask You to take my mind off the director's chair and put it in its rightful place. Forgive me, Lord, for the arrogance of thinking that Your voice to me was meaningless. I release to You the way I have depended upon my mind; I choose to depend upon You. Amen.

HEART BLOCK

David and I have been in church services where someone gave a prophetic word that was something like "God loves you and wants you to open your heart to Him; He is there for you. He wants to enfold you in His arms." Maybe you have heard these too! After you hear that a bazillion times, you cynically begin to think, "OK, that is just another one of those words coming from someone's heart." When we asked the Lord, "Why am I hearing that same message over and over again?" His response was, "Because you don't believe it yet." Ouch! We no longer disregard those words. Rather, we ask the Lord to forgive us for not receiving them and automatically thinking that they came from someone's heart instead of the Holy Spirit. In fact, it is Jesus saying, "I still want you to know that I love you." David and I have been married for 40 years. I still enjoy hearing him say he loves me! I wonder why our attitude is different toward God. Many choose to close the heart to simple words of love.

This process of closing the heart is one of the key blockages to hearing more from God, to experiencing the presence of Jesus, to having the very thing you want. Too many people walk through life saying, "Come, Lord! Come, Lord, No don't, no don't come too close." That is why He keeps giving the message to open your hearts. But, how can you keep your heart open?

The first thing to do is to change your attitude about words of love as coming from Him.

 Lord Jesus, I repent of all the ways I have literally discarded words coming from You because they were simple messages of love. I thought Your voice had to be complicated! Somehow, it had to be something much different. Father, forgive me when I shut out and discard Your simple messages of love. Help me open my heart to Your love. As I go through this material, I ask that You restore my ability to receive from You. Amen.

Secondly, develop your relationship with Jesus. Coming close to Him is coming into intimacy; you cannot abide in Him without intimacy. If you are honest, intimacy may scare you because of past experiences. We have all had relationships in which we have been hurt, times when we needed intimacy, but got something else. There may have been times when you needed love and closeness and Mom's response was, "I'm too busy. Go away." Her responses may have been downright hostile and mean, maybe even abusive. There may have been times when you wanted intimacy with Dad and wanted to share your heart. "Dad, I need your help; I need you to know what is going on in my life." Rather than taking time to be with you and listen, he responded with, "No, I'm not ready to spend time with you." He may have backhanded you or worse. Consequently, you now expect that kind of reaction to come from life and from God.

You can choose from several defenses when you are hurt. You can become angry, lash out in rage, and hit people or things. You can scream and do many things, but your most basic defense is to close your heart. This is both a tangible and intangible thing. You shut off; you are not going to go that way. If you ask for intimacy from someone 20 to 30 times and never receive it tangibly, you stop asking. The sad thing is that, intangibly, most often you put that expectation on God. If you did not receive a positive response to overtures of intimacy when you were a child, you may come to God expecting that He will not meet you or be there for you. Closing the heart makes it even harder to hear Him. I know of not one prayer that will dissolve all your expectations or a simple remedy for all of the ways you may have closed off your heart because of childhood experiences. You can pray generally through some of the most common ones, and that helps. But if you sense that you are not finished, find someone for one-on-one prayer ministry.

Sometimes you have to play detective in your life by asking, "Lord, what is stopping me from opening my heart? Why is something stopping me, and where did it come from?" Every time He shows you your bitter root of judgment or expectation and where it came from, you can forgive the people who tempted you to judge and receive release from false expectations.

 Lord Jesus, I bring You all the pain of wounds, hurts, disappointment, and loneliness I endured and ask that You find and open the closed off places in my heart. Somewhere deep in my spirit I said, "God won't meet me either." I choose to forgive Mom, I forgive Dad, and I forgive those who were supposed to help me, but did not. I bring before You the way that I still carry this judgment that "God won't help me either." I repent of it now, in Jesus' name. I lay it at the foot of Your cross. I renounce every way I have believed that You are like my Mom or Dad. I renounce all those images, all the ways I laminated onto You what I did or did not receive that was hurtful. I ask that You bring an end to the behavior patterns that rise up in me and cause me to shut off my heart even though I may not know that I am doing it. Lord, in Jesus' name I ask that You put these behavior patterns to death on the cross right now. I desire to be open and intimate with You, to trust You. Please give me a measure of trust that I did not have before because of all the ways I shut down. Teach and keep teaching me to trust. Rebuild the fractured place in me where trust died or stopped. Rebuild it, Lord. Release truth to me. Show me what You want me to believe about You that is different from what I currently believe. Speak Your words of truth. Jesus, I am going to listen for a time right now. Please show me the lies I hold on to because of what happened so long ago. I wait before You. Amen.

If the Lord reveals resentment in the quiet, you can forgive if you know the kind of circumstance it came from. You can speak aloud or silently in your heart, "I renounce that Lord because it is not true of You." Journaling what you heard in the silence is helpful because later you can read and ponder what the Lord said. A written account becomes a reference point.

"I Can't!"

You may believe that you "can't." Perhaps you need a healing of your will. Many people define prayer ministry as healing the emotions, and certainly there is a lot of emotional as well as spiritual stuff that happens in prayer ministry, but you may need a basic level of healing of your will as well. When you were growing up or even as an adult, you may have had experiences in which you were unable to make any difference in your circumstances. Nothing you did or said changed anything. You were constantly up against a situation that you could not change or some person who had a stronger, more domineering, more controlling will than you. It is easy for adults to control and dominate a child. When you were a child, you may never have had choices, even within your limited sphere.

A grandmother told of taking her 3-year-old grandson shopping for a jacket because of the cold weather. As they were shopping, she realized that he had an opinion about the kind of jacket he wanted—at the age of 3½! The Lord spoke to her and said, "You weren't given a choice when you were little so you didn't know that little children actually have opinions and want to make their own choices. But I created you to have choices from the very beginning." If you did not have the opportunity to choose, you did not develop that ability. The ability to choose is also essential to decision making. If you have trouble making decisions, look at that difficulty from your history of making choices. If a child does not develop the ability to choose, decision-making as an adult can be difficult.

> *This day I call heaven and earth as witnesses against you that I have set before you life and death, blessings and curses. Now choose life, so that you and your children may live, and that you may love the Lord your God, listen to His voice and hold fast to Him. For the Lord is your life…* (Deuteronomy 30:19-20)

Again, today the Lord says to you, "Choose life!" If you feel you were not given choices or the opportunity to develop the ability to make choices, the Lord wants to restore that to you. Jesus said, *"But blessed are your eyes because they see, and your ears because they hear"* (Matt. 13:16). And I would add, blessed is your will because you can choose. The Lord would not say, "Choose life," if He had not given you the ability to choose.

 Lord Jesus, I bring before You all the ways I was overcome by others who made all my choices for me. I forgive them and release those who took away my ability to choose. I repent for judging them. I repent for abdicating the responsibility to learn to choose. I reclaim the right to choose life. I reclaim the right to have You restore my will and my ability to choose. I ask that You strengthen me and restore that to me now. Pour strength back into me in the area of my will so that I can choose godly things, choose life, choose You, and know that I have a will. I renounce all the times when I have said, "I give up, and I can't."

The Lord does want you to surrender to Him, but that is not the same thing as "giving in." Surrendering to Him involves enlisting your reasoning capacity to help enable you to buy into and align with His ways. It is allowing His righteousness to be in charge, while at the same time being His partner in the continued molding process. It is acknowledging His ways, laying yours aside, and voluntarily committing to learning His ways. Giving in is passively acquiescing like a mindless robot, which is not at all what God wants you to do.

 Lord, any way that the word surrender has been mixed up, I ask You to remove the distortion. Surrender means using my will to accept and walk in Your ways, not having no will at all! I choose to accept Your ways.

People who abdicate their personal will tend to end up not only giving in, but giving up as well. As you reclaim your will, you might have to choose to shake off the futility that has come from not using it and replace futility with faith. Lyn had a dream in which she was supposed to go to a church camp for a weekend. She arrived expecting to have a wonderful time. Instead, it felt like she was in a prisoner of war camp. She walked around the barbed wire enclosure trying to remember all the rules thinking, "My goodness, how am I going to get out of here? I don't want to be here!" She felt powerless because she was stuck in this place with no idea of how to escape. In the middle of her dilemma, the Holy Spirit, like a spear through her mind, said, "I can pray. I can pray." It was so powerful that she woke up with those words in her mind. She knew that, for her, the Spirit of God was saying that she is never *"stuck."*

 Lord, I ask You to restore belief that prayer is powerful. It is not powerless; it is full of power. I ask You to fill me with the faith to believe it is powerful and that something is happening in my human spirit, even

if I can see nothing with my natural eye. When the time is right, many things will happen because I prayed, and for that, I thank You.

GENERATIONAL OR CHURCH ISSUES

Belief systems in your heritage that you have embraced can block your hearing. Ask the Lord what those belief systems are, since they may still influence you. Every culture has some kind of belief in its generational heritage that in some way blocks ability to hear God.

David and I have prayed with people from England, Ireland, and Wales who felt that God was aloof. God was "up there," not "down here." This cultural perspective created a separation between the people and God. Individuals wanting to see and experience God differently prayed with us thoroughly over that perspective and renounced it. North American culture teaches the belief that you have to rely on yourself. There is also a generational aspect as each generation actively participates in living that belief. In some cases, a belief can be both cultural and generational. Wisdom says to look from both perspectives and pray what the Lord shows you to pray.

The Finnish culture has a saying, "After the joy comes the tears." However, Scripture says, *"Those who sow in tears will reap with songs of joy"* (Ps. 126:5). Ukrainian culture is very strong on the idea that bad things will always happen. A century of oppression ingrained those powerful expectations in them. Over time, expectations morphed into cultural beliefs that God *wants* bad things to happen! It seems true to them that God wants them to continue to suffer. Gloria Roberts'[1] heritage is Ukrainian, and when she taught for Elijah House in the Ukraine, she repeatedly said, "No, I don't think so. It has been that way, but it is not that God *wants* your life to be that way. He has never wanted it to be that way nor does He want it to be that way in the future." You need to renounce old cultural beliefs to receive new expectations.

You can carry beliefs from your church as well. For example, some people embrace the belief that "God doesn't talk to women" or that "the Holy Spirit is for Jesus, but not for us people." Another example is the confusion that has developed in some because of derogatory things churches have said about other denominations. You can find people in these "lesser" denominations who are godly, and some who are not, which causes confusion, and you wonder what is true. Is God with them, or is He not?

Robert told us that when he was growing up his church community did not believe the Holy Spirit was someone he could hear from directly. Rather, that community believed that God was authoritative, judgmental, and harsh. He used to think that if he ever saw God, God would be in a car with a blue flashing light, chasing him down! These cultural, generational, and church beliefs are sometimes quite subtle and held deep inside; you may not even know they are there. They do not accurately reflect the character and nature of God, but they can have a profound effect on what and how you hear God speak to you.

If you had Robert's background and heard a harsh, critical, and judgmental response from the Lord to a question or a prayer about another church, would you know that response was not from Him? Would you know that that attitude and tone was most likely coming from you and your history rather than the Lord? If you are not really walking with Jesus, or if you are, but you have not yet learned His character, you are apt to think that it came from Him. You will think that your judgmental attitude toward what is going on in another person or church comes from God because you learned that God was judgmental and harsh. It is important to immerse yourself in God's presence, to soak in what the true character of God is. Although He is righteous and holy, He is not judgmental and rarely harsh. He does not normally come at you that way. Those are two very different concepts.

You will need to develop the habit of checking your attitudes. Be sensitive to see where attitudes originate, and do not be quick to come to hard and fast conclusions when you have this sort of inheritance. Develop the reflex of aligning your thoughts with Jesus' thoughts. Ask yourself if Jesus would think this way, if Jesus would come to this conclusion, or if He would say the things you are saying.

Jesus, I pray that You would put the cross between my generational heritage and me. Stop the ungodly influences in my heritage that lied to me about who You are. I bless my heritage for the godly influences and thank You for them. I release the truth that (for instance) *You want to speak to women as much as to men. Lord, You do not judge first; You love first. I release the truth* (for instance) *that bad things will not always happen just because they happened in the past. Your will is not that I suffer intolerably. Lord, in all the ways that churches and ancestors distorted Your character, I ask for Your healing. Heal me and release to me the new thing You are doing. Amen.*

EXPECTATIONS

Projection can greatly interfere with hearing God. Unfortunately, everyone does it. You project past experiences onto others and expect them to behave accordingly. You expect that God will respond to you like your earthly father. If your earthly father was nurturing and complimentary, you may expect the same from your heavenly Father. If he was cold, angry, and sarcastic, you may expect the same from God. If he was harsh and critical, you expect the same from God. You may consciously protest that God is good and loving, but your heart believes otherwise. Do you look forward to time with Him, or do you quickly become distracted? Are Scripture reading, worship, and prayer a joy or a chore? You may unconsciously attach any judgment or expectation of your parents, caregivers, and authority figures to God. That can make it difficult to hear God's voice. To you, it may sound an awful lot like Dad. I met a couple of individuals who prayed desperately to hear God and could not because they made inner vows in childhood. They determined that they would not listen to their fathers who were violent, abusive brutes. When they faced and repented of their hatred of their fathers' violence, they could hear God clearly.

Some people are not sure it is OK to hear from God directly. They have had bad experiences sharing what they heard with an authority figure. The person in authority squelched them and did not allow them to speak of their experiences in the church setting. You may have witnessed a friend who was hurt in this fashion, and from that experience, you developed an expectation that others will minimize, dismiss, or reject what you share. You may have concluded that hearing from God is bad and hurtful, rather than seeing that it was the people's reactions that were bad and hurtful.

Another expectation that can block your hearing is that God speaks in a "stained glass" voice. Some believe His voice will sound very different from theirs or that He will only use King James English. In some 50 plus years of knowing Christ, I have met only one person who heard God speak to her in that dialect, and David has only met one! It got that person's attention! Because the Lord meets you where you are, normally, His voice does not sound so different from your own.

David became acquainted with a young pastor named Brad, mentioned earlier. At a seminar, Brad shared that a friend came to him and asked why he did not hear the voice of Jesus. The friend maintained that he simply could not hear Jesus' voice. A Scripture from Job immediately came into Brad's mind. It was from the speech of Elihu, the one good counselor out of the four friends who came to visit him in his distress. He said, *"Why do you complain to Him that He answers none of man's words. For God does speak—now one way, now another—though man may not perceive it"* (Job 33:14). Brad realized that God was saying that He was speaking to this man in many ways, whether he perceived it or not.

Perhaps you could say that God's voice is "there" in the way that radio waves are "there." It is not true that God does not speak to you. Psalm 139:17 says, *"How precious to me are Your thoughts, O God! How vast is the sum of them."* You need to begin to receive His thoughts. Being able to hear God's thoughts about burdens and to trust that you hear accurately greatly reduces the weight and unnecessary cost of burden bearing.

The Psalmist says, *"...The things You planned for us no one can recount to You; were I to speak and tell of them, they would be too many to declare"* (Ps. 40:5). God is thinking and planning for you continually! If you occupy His thoughts to that extent, it would follow that He also speaks to you. You may believe God is communicating, but too often you may fail to recognize God as the author of what you are receiving! As I have said, many times your expectations of what God is like reflect your relationship with your earthly father. You can ask Him to teach you His character, to give you accurate pictures of Himself. This will result in a mind shift away from thinking of a God who is distant and disconnected from creation, away from the image of one who sits on a cloud with a fly swatter, waiting to thump you on the head if you mess up or have fun.

FEAR

A pastor's son asked for prayer. He was about 19, he was leaving for college, and he was afraid. We sat down and asked the Lord where the fear came from. What came immediately to his mind was the memory of standing on the church steps, locked outside, waiting for his dad to come back. On that particular Sunday his dad forgot, drove home, and began to have lunch. A half hour later he finally remembered, "Oh, oh! John is not with us!" He returned and found his son lonely, forlorn, and not knowing what to do. That memory came back to him powerfully. It is important not only to ask the Lord where your fear came from, but also to ask, "What did I *believe* as a result of that experience?" We asked the Lord what belief came out of it.

His belief was that his father would not remember him, but would leave him behind. A bit of trust died in him that day. He could not be sure he could depend upon dad. Now that he was leaving for college, could he depend upon God? John developed an expectation that if his dad forgot him, God would also forget him. He forgave his dad for forgetting him and broke the power of the belief that "God will forget me." You may have similar feelings because you were left or forgotten somewhere and fear took root.

Just as there are veins of gold through rock, veins of fear can spread through your life. Address fears because the Lord wants you to walk in His perfect peace. To do that you must find where the fear began, forgive those involved in the experiences that caused the fear, and repent of judging them. Ask the Lord for His truth and peace to calm your mind and emotions so you can walk with Him in joy.

Sometimes demons energize a fear, making it even worse. This is not to say that a person is necessarily possessed or inhabited; he may be harassed from a distance. Being near a messenger of the enemy can crank up fear, whatever that fear may be. Praying forgiveness and repentance for the source of the fear removes what demons see as their legal right to harass you. You can then bind the demons and send them away. *"And these signs will accompany those who have believed: In My name they will cast out demons..."* (Mark 16:17 NASB). Ask the Lord to fill or cover the point of harassment. The demons will not come back because there will be no place for them to attach (see Luke 11:24-26).

Fear can rise up because of any kind of abuse. As a child, when you were hurt in any way, you were powerless to stop it so you may have developed a fear that this would happen again. The message is, "There is no protection for me." That was a big one for Grace[2] because there was a time when her mother became unbalanced and hostile. She remembers her mother beating her when she was about three. She lived with fear as a result. When she received healing for the effects of the physical abuse, the fear left and peace stayed. Peace became a constant in her life, whereas before, it would come and go. Fear had always arisen and crowded it out.

Jesus does not want you to have fear. If fear rises up when you ask Him to speak to you, do not run away. Rather, ask, "Lord, why am I fearful? What is going on?" As you locate your fears, it is good to ask the following questions: 1) "Where did it come from?" and

2) "What did I believe because of the experience?" Did you believe that there was no real protection? Jesus can be your protector as well as your Savior—ask Him to be. Scripture says repeatedly that He is your refuge, He is your place of safety, and you can hide in Him. He gives these pictures of protection because He actually intends to protect you. Jesus has an abundance of good things to give, but if you do not believe that He will, you will not feel the benefits.

Lord, where fear has taken up residence, I ask that You search it out and bind it so that it has no more effect in my life. Wash it out of me. Put it on Your cross and cause Your perfect peace to flow back into me—peace that is the opposite of fear and anxiety, the perfect peace that You have for me. Wherever I was powerless and believed that there was no protection, I give You that belief. I ask You to come and stand in the place where I was hurt and unprotected. Lord Jesus, come as my protector. Speak to my heart and human spirit right now. I ask You to witness to me by Your Holy Spirit that You can stand in that place of hurt and be my protection. Amen.

SHAME

Shame not only interferes with hearing God, it also cloaks your heart and severely impairs your ability to believe anything good you hear. Shame makes it especially hard to hear good about yourself. David and I invited a woman to "see" Jesus or sense His presence or allow Him to meet her in whatever other way He chose as we prayed with her. We waited for a few minutes and asked if she saw or sensed anything. She said that she saw a picture of Jesus and herself sitting on the grass, but not very close to each other. She said that her head was kind of down as if she did not want to look at Him. We asked why she did not want to look at Jesus and what came to her mind immediately were the words, "I am really, really bad."

Shame makes you feel like—"I am dirty and worthless. I am somehow not right." When we asked where the shame came from, she remembered being molested by her brother. When she had told her father, he blamed her! What hurt her so deeply was not just that her brother had molested her, but the fact that her father had blamed her for it. That was why the shame settled on her spirit. She shriveled up inside and felt, "I am really, really bad. That is why this happened to me. It is my fault." We could have said, "It's not your fault," but when we asked Jesus what the truth was, *He* said, "That was not your fault." Jesus' words to her were much more powerful than ours would have been. His words set her free. Then she forgave her father as well as her brother.

Believing it was her fault was a judgment[3] upon herself. You can judge yourself as surely as you judge others. It is especially easy for a child to do. As a child, you can automatically think there must be something wrong with "me" when these things happen.

Negative Self-image

Of all the ways the Lord has of communicating with you, what you may find the hardest to trust are the thoughts in your head. They sound so like your own voice. Usually they are good, encouraging words, but you have a hard time believing good things about yourself. You tell yourself that these good thoughts tempt you into pride and conceit.

If God constantly thinks about you, plans for you, and seeks every opportunity to relate, you can assume that He will say things that will comfort you, encourage your heart, teach you His ways, and build your faith. A good father has good things to say to his children. A good father encourages and comforts his children. A good father trains his children according to his values and in ways that equip the children for making their way through life. A good father uses punishment only as a last resort. *"For if He causes grief, then He will have compassion according to His abundant loving kindness. **For He does not afflict willingly or grieve the sons of men**"* (Lam. 3:32-33 NASB). You have difficulty believing the good things God says to you and about you because you have a poorer picture of yourself than God does. God sees you as a redeemed, new creature; He sees you through the eyes of Jesus' love for you.

You feel as you do about yourself because of negative experiences with people in family, school, community, or church authority. Negative experiences taught you negative things. You came to negative conclusions when people who were supposed to teach you neglected to teach you anything about yourself, so you assumed the worst. You tend to see yourself through the filter of negative messages that became your truth. You expect God the Father to act and sound like your earthly father or mother. You have a hard time believing God will be any different from your parents if they were not complimenting or encouraging.

Weaving throughout this discussion of hearing and relating to God is the broad strand of trust. Many of the blocks to hearing from God result from a lack of trust or from broken trust. It is appropriate to look at trust and how to either build or repair it.

DISHONESTY

Be brutally honest with God; anything less diminishes your ability to hear God. Jesus wants you to speak to Him the depth of what you feel. This is for your benefit; He already knows your hidden thoughts because He is God. But if you try to hide things from Him and do not want to admit what you feel, the hiding keeps you from feeling close to Him. You will be unable to have intimate conversations with Him. Imagine trying to converse with a best friend or spouse, but never being honest about what you feel. It could not be a very productive or satisfying conversation! It is necessary to come to the point where you can honestly confess your pains to the Lord. When you talk with people and hear that they are unable to hear the Lord's wisdom for their circumstances, ask the Lord to reveal to them what is stopping them or us from hearing. Usually what happens is that out of the mouth comes a rush of feelings. "Well, this is what happened to me, and nobody understands how bad it was!"

A pastor told of a time when he was praying with a woman and both were unable to hear from the Lord. They came to a memory of something bad that had happened, but could not access God at all. They asked what was still in the way. Out from her lips came, "I hate God! He wasn't there for me." After that, they were able to hear Jesus.

When you finally confess what is really in your heart, it does not stop God from connecting with you. He knows how to handle emotions. You can literally give Him your hate, and He will take it away. You can give Him your anger, and He can take it away. But until you confess it, you cannot give it to Him. If you do not confess it, He will not take it from you. Scripture says you must *"Be angry, and yet do not sin..."* (Eph. 4:26 NASB), before it says, *"Let all…anger…be put away from you…"* (Eph. 4:31). You must have honesty in your relationship with God. It really helps to learn that early in your Christian walk.

You may need to repent of a number of judgments that developed when you were growing up. Who in your life did not want you to be honest? You may need to ask the Lord to forgive you for believing that He is like your mother, father, or some authority figure with whom it was better and safer not to tell the truth.

STRONGHOLDS

Strongholds[4] are powerful blocks to your hearing from God. A stronghold is a practiced way of thinking *that takes you away from truth.* For instance, many who try to hear God become frustrated. My husband's definition of frustration is "what we feel when we are not able to have our own way." You become frustrated when you try to do something, believing you are "on God's side." You are trying to do God's thing, and for the nineteenth time you are blocked! AAAAGH! After frustration comes discouragement. If you let that continue, after discouragement comes depression—the Quick Response Team of Rude Philistines has arrived! If you entertain depression long enough, you fall into complete defeat, to the point of giving up.

Another practiced way of thinking starts with anger. You are trying to do something and encounter a blockage, or someone does something that angers you. You attack or withdraw; once withdrawn you blame. "You made me do this; you made me angry. You made me go away pouting." Then when the Holy Spirit starts to convict, you enter into self-blame. "I'm no good; I'm a lousy husband, a lousy father," and that leads to self-hate. Self-hate can be a stronghold too. Once you develop the habit patterns that conduct you through this cyclic, structured way of thinking, they kidnap you away from truth and away from God. It is difficult to hear from God when you are in this cycle. A friend of ours calls this "circling the drain!" It will suck you down if you let it.

The Lord has revealed to us that you have to stop the thought process at the beginning. If you let your thinking go down through these cycles, you become stuck in emotions and it takes longer and is much harder to come out. When you become frustrated, sin is right there—the rude Philistines, Unbelief and Lack of Trust, are waiting for you. When you react in anger, that reaction is sin. You cannot allow yourself to fall into discouragement and then depression, defeat, or self-blame. Ask the Lord to reveal the root of frustration. Where does that come from? Why are you stuck in frustration?

We asked God these questions, and in a still small voice He said, "You are stuck because you don't really trust that I will do anything about your situation. You cannot do anything about it. You are blocked; you have tried, and nothing you did worked, so you think, *I am the one who is blocked.*" So then we asked the Lord what to do. It came down to repenting for all the ways we believed God was powerless. Because we were powerless to accomplish something or could not do things the way we wanted, at heart level, we believed God was powerless also.

Something can happen to you when, as children, you see people in pain and no one helps. Something can rise up in you that says, "No one else is helping all these people. I have to do it." Consequently, you become the savior of the world. Many have to resign from that post because Savior is Jesus' job. If you are honest, you have to admit that you are not doing a very good job of it. Some people have to resign more than once. It amazes David that every time he resigns, the Lord accepts his resignation—every time!

Taking on the savior-of-the-world identity comes out of a lack of trust at a foundational level. That lack of trust impels you through these patterns of thinking.

If you have this struggle, you will need to come to see that deep in your inner being you believe God does not have the power that you need to overcome, to help others, or to do the things that need doing. Keep asking the Lord for increased ability to trust Him. Whenever He shows you an area of life in which you do not trust, keep forgiving all the people in your life who did not model trust to you. God gave you parents. He gave them the responsibility of teaching you truth and teaching you about God. Many have, or had, parents who did not fulfill that responsibility. To the extent that you reacted to that lack, you have to continue to forgive and release; keep asking God to heal those places so you can fully trust Him.

All the burden bearers I know have a deep desire to trust God fully, completely, and entirely. They desire that trust be so strong that circumstances cannot overwhelm. Total trust is the goal. I know of no one who feels he has arrived! For example, you may come into a time when money is scarce, and you go into distress. But you do not have to become distressed because God is healing you of the thought pattern that leads you to feel overwhelmed. You can stand and say, "No, Jesus is my provider. True, money is scarce now, but it won't always be." The way to remove these strongholds of thought and retrain the mind is to continue to forgive those who were not there for you in the ways you needed them to be and to repent for judgments against them. Having forgiven, continue to ask God to heal your trust and help you develop new thought patterns. It also helps to have a friend to call when you find yourself catastrophising.

Disappointment With God

Disappointment is a serious block. At one time or another, just about everyone feels like this. It is as though you bought a ticket to Hawaii. You packed your bags, including your bathing suit, bright beach towel, and fancy plastic drink cups. You boarded the plane, but when you deplaned—you were in Barrow, Alaska! There were no beaches and not much sun. You arrived at an entirely different place. Life looks very different from what you originally thought it was going to look like. The place where you are is not what you planned, yet here you are.

To compound that, there are ways that God uses the trials and testing in your life to strengthen you. From a human perspective, you may seem to grow weaker because of these times. People who do not have God may depend on addictions, needing drugs, alcohol, or something else to help them through extremely hard times and difficult circumstances. These trials and troubles might actually make them weaker, but as a Christian, you have God. He will use the hard things in your life to strengthen you.

However, if you are not careful, when you experience the hard times, you can become so weary that you begin to lose hope and perspective about what God is doing or what He is like. What can you look forward to? Why are you in "Barrow, Alaska" instead of "Hawaii?" Can you make a life here in Alaska? Are you going to live the rest of your life looking for the runway—a way out? When is the plane coming? Does God even live here? Yes, He does.

In a prophetic word, Bob Jones talked about how individuals, churches, and movements have been barren for an extended season.[5] Nothing has seemed to bear much fruit. But at the appointed time, individuals, churches and movements will bear fruit. He referred to

Romans 4:19-20 that described Abraham's faith which overcame barrenness. We have profound promises to overcome disappointments and seasons of barrenness such as in Romans 9:9, *"At the appointed time I will return, and Sarah will have a son."*

We believe that God uses hard times in your life to strengthen you so that you will be able to stand what is coming. More of the Holy Spirit is coming, and with Him always comes spiritual warfare. They go together. You will need to be able to stand in the warfare to accept what the Holy Spirit is doing. You may experience disappointment with God to the extent that you feel weary or feel unable to look to the future because the past has been so difficult. Sometimes you are angry with God, and other times you hold pain toward God. You thought God was going to do one thing, but that was not what He did. His warning is:

"For My thoughts are not your thoughts, neither are your ways My ways," declares the Lord. "As the heavens are higher than the earth, so are My ways higher than your ways and My thoughts than your thoughts" (Isaiah 55:8-9).

Behind this kind of painful weariness, there can be severe disappointment because of what you thought God was going to do, but He did not do it. Someone said, "I am so tired of hearing what God is *going* to do."

 Father, I have become tired because I have been hearing what You are going to do but have yet to see it. I feel that I have boarded a plane, expecting to deplane on a beach, but instead have landed on ice. Holy Spirit, come powerfully to me right now. Come and release every place in me that carries disappointment because of the outcome of my circumstances. Release me, Lord. Meet me at

*the cross and lift off the weariness of the journey, the tiredness, and
the disappointment that not as much has happened as I was hoping
and that I am not in the place that I expected to be. Lord Jesus, take
all of that. Where there are generational deposits in which there is
weariness that I have absorbed from my parents, Lord take it all.
Release into me the knowledge that I am in the right place, that You
brought me here! This is where You intended me to be. So, Lord,
help me set my heart and will, and help me declare that the place
where I am now is OK because You are going to ensure that I arrive
where You want me to be. Release hope, hope, and more hope.
Forgive me for any way in which I have looked at You through eyes
of criticism, cynicism, or unbelief because what I hoped for did not
match what I saw. Forgive me, Lord, for that. I declare that You are
good. You are just, You are wise, and You are Lord. I declare that You
intend to bring me good things. Amen.*

BURDENS CARRIED NEEDLESSLY

You carry two kinds of personal burdens, truth-based and lie-
based. The basis for guilt and shame can be either truth or a lie. Truth-
based guilt would be for something you actually did that was wrong.
If you did something wrong, you are guilty and need to confess it and
ask God to forgive you. You can and need to resolve and release such
guilt to the Lord. He came to forgive and release you.

As a young adult, sometimes Gloria Roberts would say to
her brother, a psychologist, "I really should not do this because
of that." He would look at her and say, "You know, there isn't
quite enough guilt there. Do you think you could generate some
more?"

Guilt is a gift of God as long as you bring it to the Lord and confess what you have done—then He can release you from it. Shame, however, comes not from what you have done, but what you believe: "I am bad. I am unworthy." Although not true, it somehow too often has become your identity. You cannot confess shame because it is not based on something you did that was wrong. You do not have to carry shame; you can ask Jesus to lift it from you and teach you truth. Shame is a burden you carry needlessly.

 Lord, wash through me and lift off deposits of shame. Wash off the places of shame that came through no fault of my own. It came through my agreement with the labels, actions, and the things that other people said and did. Lord, break the power of guilt and shame now. Lift and release every deposit of shame. I ask that You put it on Your cross. Lord, replace shame with more of Your love and acceptance. Replace it with the truth that You created me and love me. Amen.

Other emotions can come between you and God, which underscores the need to be honest with God. If you are grieving because you lost someone, you can bring that grief to the Lord and release that person's care to the Lord. Or you can grieve about whatever you have lost, material worth, job, reputation, and so forth. Ask Him to come and remove the excess grief so that you do not have to carry the weight of all of it. You grieve because you are human, but you do not have to grieve forever.

Anger is another emotion that can interfere with your ability to hear God. If you are carrying anger, the base of anger is usually hurt. People do not become angry in a vacuum. If you are angry, you can say, *"Lord, I'm angry because this is what happened to me, but I don't want to carry this anger anymore, and I am willing to release it to You. I confess that carrying it for years and years is a sin, and I do not want that. I release it to You, Lord. Will you take it?"* He will take your anger.

Sometimes emotions are based on judgments or inner vows rather than on truth. For instance, if you feel hopeless or if you feel despair, that may have been preceded by anger because something happened to you. However, hopelessness and despair come from *the bitter root expectation* that you will always be in that place of pain—that there is no hope for the future. You have believed something that is not true. There is a big difference between being angry because something really happened to you and feeling despair or hopelessness because you *believe* it will never be any different. God says, *"It will be different!"* It will be different because He has plans for you that give you hope and a future (see Jer. 29:11).

You may carry loneliness because of a trauma that needs to be resolved. If you continue to feel intense loneliness after ministry to the trauma, then you can know that you do not really believe Jesus' words, *"I am with you always"* (Matt. 28:20; also see Deut. 31:6). Jesus came to fill your loneliness as well as to give you salvation. Feelings of despair, loneliness, fear, anxiety, and powerlessness can be lie-based pain. You may believe that things will never be better, that no one will ever protect you, and other false things about the future. They are not the truth.

STRONG PERSONAL DESIRES

Strong personal desires can wreak havoc on your discernment. Ezekiel 14:4 says that if a person has an idol in his heart, the Lord will *"answer him...in keeping with his great idolatry."* In other words, if you want a Porsche and keep saying to the Lord, "I want this. Will you give it to me?" you will probably think you hear "yes" because that is what you want to hear. Some call this "blab it and grab it" faith. What you want clouds your ability to hear correctly. It is as if the Lord stands back and says, "Sure, go ahead. That's what you are going to do anyway." Everyone does this to some degree at one time or another, but you miss the good that God planned for you when this happens.

What is the way out of this mess? How can you find clarity? If there is anything in you that already wants to hear a certain answer or go a certain way, pray this, *"Lord Jesus, I lay on Your altar all my desires, all the ways that I want to go."* You may even imagine putting this desire on the altar, saying, *"I do not want my own desire in this matter! Take it Lord. Let it kick and scream, but take it. I know that in my heart there are things I want to hear."*

This is particularly important when you pray for direction. It is not so important when you pray for healing, because Scripture is very clear—Jesus wants to heal. The same is true when praying for encouragement. Jesus wants to encourage you. However, what you already want to hear, or what you think God wants you to hear, can cloud your prayers for direction! For example, you may say, "Obviously, He wants our church to hire 10 more staff members by next year because look at all the hurting people! Our job is to find the staff!" Not necessarily. Even your desire to help can cloud your hearing. Again, pray this way: *Lord, I lay all my desires on Your altar. I lay them down and ask You to take them so I can hear You.*

The more you do this, the more you will hear clearly because God honors that prayer. If you do not pray that way, you will sometimes hear directions from your own heart and your own desires. Upon first reading, that Scripture in Ezekiel can be very scary! The way out is to lay your desires down by an act of your will.

During 2001, Gwynne went through a time when it seemed as though she was around so many hopeless people that the hopelessness affected her. One of the things that influenced her strongly was that someone close to her had been sick for a long time and the caregiving was taking its toll. She began to cry, plead, and pray to the Lord, "Please God, heal this woman and do it this year because I don't think I can carry on with this situation after Christmas. *It has to be this year.*" November came and the woman was not well, and Gwynne's hope died. She thought that wellness was never going to happen. It was already November and Christmas was around the corner, and she felt she absolutely could not do any more.

At about that time she read a newspaper article, an interview with a POW who had been in Vietnam for eight years. The journalist asked how he had survived. He said that it was interesting how some people came into the camp and said, "I will be out by Christmas," or "I will be out by Thanksgiving," and when they weren't, they went into despair and some of them died. The POW kept himself alive with the hope that "I will eventually be released." He said, "Never let the tyranny of your present circumstances rob you of your faith in your ultimate victory." Applying this story to your own life, you can say, "I will not let what is happening now prevent me from believing that God will ultimately bring me victory."

Deadlines are deadly. God is not obligated to operate according to your deadline. If you say to God, "I can't do this anymore," you are making a lie of the Scripture that says, *"My grace is sufficient for you"* (2 Cor. 12:9). You can honestly say, "God I don't know how I can do this anymore" and invite Him to strengthen you. Ask Him to enlarge your capacity. Seek help and be honest, but if you make a blanket statement and say, "I can't do this anymore," then you are not allowing God to help you, and you are agreeing with the enemy that this life is too much. You cannot hear God when the enemy has your ears!

BITTERNESS

Bitterness can be a way of life, and severe hurts can be very difficult to forgive. A woman who was working on forgiving her husband for something for the eighty-fifth time was talking to a friend. She said, "I cannot seem to let this go. I cannot seem to release it. I am still holding onto it. What is the matter?" As they prayed, the Lord said, "You need to repent of holding on." So she said, "Lord, forgive me. I am powerless to release this thing to you. This bitterness is so deep in my heart I can't even give it to you, so would you forgive me for holding onto the bitterness?" That was when He took it away.

You may say the words, "I forgive you," to people, but then put yourself in a place of being over them. "They hurt me, and now I am such a big person; I forgive them and release them." But what if you still hold onto the notion that you have been hurt and are still bitter about it? You can say the words, "I forgive you," but until you see that your own bitterness is a sin and confess it as such, God will not release you from it. Your forgiveness of the other will not be complete. It will be empty words.

If someone hurts you and you forgive her instantly, before there is any bitterness, then "I forgive you" might be adequate and appropriate because bitterness did not have time to lodge in the heart. That is the best way to try to live life. Forgive in the moment; that is what Jesus did. While He was dying on the cross, He said, *"Father, forgive them..."* (Luke 23:34). He is your model; forgive as soon as you possibly can. If you have been hurt a while ago and are still holding onto pain, bitterness causes you to hold on. Release bitterness because it comes between you and the Lord and destroys your peace. In the end, those who caused hurt and those who were hurt stand together at the cross, evenly.

You will have to walk in twice as much grace and forgiveness as normal if there is someone in the family who continues to have a problem with the one who caused the hurt. You have to forgive and be careful because the bitterness of the offended individual can affect and sway you even after you forgive. Be up front with the Lord and constantly forgive.

Blessing is also good. It is the last step in forgiveness. Like a grace note, it puts a finishing touch on forgiveness and is a way of assuring that you will not become bitter about that same hurt again. When you forgive, release an offence, ask the Lord to release you from bitterness, and bless the person who hurt you—then you have moved around the full circle. You have allowed the Lord to do His full work in you when you bless and return love to those who hurt you. It is all about love. God says that the world will know Christians by their love and unity (see John 17:21).

Father, thank You for the pounds of weight You have lifted off as I have prayed throughout this chapter. Lord, as You spoke powerfully through that little newspaper article about the POW, speak powerfully to me. I need to hear that truth right now. I need to know that there will be an ultimate victory and that You give me the ability to stand and wait for it. You have. So, Lord, I give You the times when in my heart I felt like I could not go on or when I gave You a deadline or made a demand, Lord. Increase my strength, stamina, and capacity. Increase my belief that there will be an eventual victory, that prayers are powerful, and that ultimately I will win. I know I am on the winning side, regardless of how it feels. Continue to open my spiritual eyes and ears—the eyes and ears of my heart. Open my heart wherever it is closed so that I see You, hear You, and love You. Amen

You will encounter other blocks and difficulties as you walk with God. I encourage you to dialog with God continuously in order to move past stalemates. Sometimes you will need to have some human help as well, but many things you can do completely on your own with the Lord.

Negative Self-image

Of all the ways the Lord has of communicating with you, what you may find the hardest to trust are the thoughts in your head. They sound so like your own voice. Usually they are good, encouraging words, but you have a hard time believing good things about yourself. You tell yourself that these good thoughts tempt you into pride and conceit.

If God constantly thinks about you, plans for you, and seeks every opportunity to relate, you can assume that He will say things that will comfort you, encourage your heart, teach you His ways, and build your faith. A good father has good things to say to his children. A good father encourages and comforts his children. A good father trains his children according to his values, and in ways that equip the children for making their way through life. A good father uses punishment only as a last resort. *"For if He causes grief, then He will have compassion according to His abundant loving kindness. **For He does not afflict willingly or grieve the sons of men**"* (Lam. 3:32-33 NASB). You have difficulty believing the good things God says to you and about you because you have a poorer picture of yourself than God does. God sees you as a redeemed, new creature; He sees you through the eyes of Jesus' love for you.

You feel as you do about yourself because of negative experiences with people in family, school, community, or church authority.

Negative experiences taught you negative things. You came to negative conclusions when people who were supposed to teach you neglected to teach you anything about yourself, so you assumed the worst. You tend see yourself through the filter of negative messages that became your truth. You expect God the Father to act and sound like your earthly father or mother. You have a hard time believing God will be any different from your parents if they were not complimenting or encouraging.

Weaving throughout this discussion of hearing and relating to God is the broad strand of trust. Many of the blocks to hearing from God result from a lack of trust or from broken trust. It is appropriate to look at trust and how to either build or repair it.

ENDNOTES

1. Gloria Roberts is the founder of Elijah House, Canada.

2. Fictional name—the actual names of individuals are always changed to protect privacy. If this is your story and your name, it is purely coincidental!

3. See *The Mystery of Spiritual Sensitivity*, Chapter 4, for a fuller explanation of judgments and inner vows.

4. An ungodly habit that has a strong hold on you. You can have a stronghold in thinking or behavior.

5. Bob Jones, http://www.bobjones.org/Docs/ShepherdsRod2006.htm

CHAPTER 7

The Issue of Trust

H*AVING DISCUSSED HEARING OR NOT* hearing from God, I can hear an echo, "Yeah, right! Like I could hear God! Like He would talk to me!" and other such sentiments. I know some are having this reaction because I had it too! Hearing from God involves trust, and for far too many highly sensitive people, trust is in short supply or has been shattered altogether. To understand how to repair shattered trust, let us first look at how to build foundational trust.

BUILDING BASIC TRUST

One of the first developmental tasks an infant has is to develop basic trust.[1] Trust builds when an infant is consistently cared for lovingly and gently during the first few years of life. The child trusts as he learns the world is a safe place. A child learns trust by receiving consistently loving, gentle nurture and attention to his needs. He learns trust as a parent carries him, walks him, and talks to him, but this is learned uniquely from the father, as he feels the strength and safety of the father's arms and chest. He learns trust from loving responses and faces that communicate, "I am happy to be with you."

Lack of trust, insecurity, and anxiety come from reaction to red, angry faces and loud voices that "are not happy to be with me!" Lack of trust comes in reaction to inconsistent or mechanical feeding and handling and to the absence of emotion on faces! The child learns, "I am a bother," and "people put up with me because they have to."

An adult who learned trust as a child is able to hold the heart open, to allow another person "in," to be vulnerable. People who learn trust are able to take risks because there is a foundational knowledge that "I can venture out with another person and not lose myself;" relationships are "safe." Happy faces teach you that you have something to give and that receiving is fun. "We" is much more fun than "me!" Betrayals, persecutions, deceits, deceptions, and other such hard experiences do serious damage to trust.

REBUILDING TRUST

Relationships wound you, and relationships heal you. Seeking inner healing for your bitter reactions to the wounds you received because of your high sensitivity is the first thing you can do for yourself. The second is to find safe, comforting people who do not punish you for expressing hurt, pain, or confusion or for being different. Safe people can teach and train you in burden bearing by giving honest, consistent, and loving feedback. *Trust will facilitate learning to bear burdens in a healthy way.* You must be able to trust God and those to whom you commit yourself. Trusting is not easy, but that is precisely why a small group of **trusted** *friends* is essential. In the safety of a trusting environment, you will be able to be both student and teacher. You can share and learn from each other's struggles and victories, and you can hold each other to the goals and commitments you make. In the company of a small group of friends, all of whom are on the same journey, you can learn or relearn how to trust others, God, and yourself.

DEFINING "ACCOUNTABILITY"

Being accountable to someone does not mean that you are to practice psychic nudity! Rather, choose carefully. Identify a person you have seen praying and interceding respectfully, who is quick to listen and slow to speak, who is accurate in the spiritual things shared. Choose someone whose judgment you have come to respect and appreciate. Seek out a person with more spiritual experience and maturity in the area of burden bearing than you have. Ask that person to consider entering into an accountability relationship with you. This means that you trust her judgment in the area of burden bearing as much or more than you trust your own. You want to be able to lean on her discernment when you are confused. You need to know that you can call on her if you need to double check your hearing or if you feel overwhelmed.

Give this person permission to ask pointed questions regarding burden bearing or any other specific area of your life. Invite him to ask how you are doing, to inquire about any disciplines you have committed to or goals you have set. Give him permission to tell you when you are not acting like yourself, to tell you when you are carrying too much for too long. *But* also be sure to ask him to tell you what you do right and to encourage you as a fellow burden bearer.

Having an accountability "group" means having more than one person to whom you are accountable. At any given time, a single individual may or may not be available. Having a "group" does not mean that you have to have regular meetings, although some do choose to meet together on a regular basis. A small group of friends is your best help, but it too can become unbalanced if you are not watchful. Continue to share with your spouse if you are married, returning often to Scripture and the Lord.

Having an accountability partner of a different gender immediately poses *potential* problems—especially if you are married, but not to this "partner." Therefore, I always recommend, especially for those new to accountability, to build a "same gender" accountability group. You eliminate most (never all—but most) problems of gossip, jealousy, slander, and you do not have to take the care necessary to avoid *"the appearance of evil."* (1 Thess. 5:22 (KJV) This is not to say that it cannot be done, just that same gender groups/partners have fewer built-in hurdles and snares! Opposite gender relationships require a good deal of maturity and honoring of each other's commitments.

TESTING THE WATERS

Common sense tells you that not everyone is a safe person. You need some way of knowing who is safe and who is not. David and I suggest sharing something that *was* once painful, but now is not so painful that you would be devastated or tempted to reject your own perspective if it was not believed or received with respect. Then wait for the reaction. Do their eyes glaze over? Do they change the subject? Do they want you to stop any further expressions? Do they respond inappropriately (with laughter, a light mood, platitudes, or worse yet, sarcasm), or do they treat you with sensitivity and respect?

Possible things to share as a test might be the hurt of being called names, being punished for someone else's error, being made to wait for dad, having dad forget to come when he said he would, or an experience of prejudice. Share how you felt about something that happened long enough ago that it is no longer a driving force in your life. Nothing anyone says will greatly upset you about the test incident. You will not be devastated if someone reacts negatively or hurtfully. The reactions of the individual(s) will reveal whether or not they can be trusted with something more sensitive.

People who are faithful with a little can be trusted with more (see Luke 19:17). If they treat the "more" with love and respect, share more. Those who respond appropriately are the ones with whom you can take more steps toward building deeper relationships, leading to the kind of supportive friendships you need in your small accountability groups. It is those people you can call for help in discerning whether 1) you are hearing from the Lord or 2) you are in some way bouncing off the wall with your own stuff. They will help you discern 3) if the Lord is asking you to carry a burden and pray it through. You never need to go into a group and immediately open your heart and let everything hang out. People *earn* trust over time, not over night. A wise proverb says, "Friendship is like a good wine; it should be sipped slowly." Let time and circumstances test before you open fully. You need to see and experience love and acceptance before your heart can hope that God will respond the same way.

TRUST IS A RISK

For some, trust has been badly shattered. But a time will come when your head tells you these people are trustworthy—they have never shown themselves otherwise. At that point, you have a choice to make. Is the risk of rejection more painful than the loneliness and isolation of not trusting people and God? Is it worse than the agony of staying at a distance, of not receiving love from people and God, of being able to see and smell the food but never being able to eat it? If you want relationship more than you have words for, *make* yourself share. You cannot build trust until you risk! It is difficult, but well worth the effort.

Trust is essential if you are to learn to bear burdens rightly. You need people who truly know you and can give you feedback when you are not acting like yourself. Nothing helped me more than having a few people who could help me understand my feelings and keep me accountable. I knew I could call any one of them and share what I was sensing or feeling without being condemned. No one told me I was being an "emotional female"—again! Nor did they tell me that I "shouldn't feel that way" or "you shouldn't say those things." You need this kind of validation. These people were very healing to me.

In the early years of David's time in the pastorate, I encountered people who refused to hear me. Neither he nor I had any idea of the weight and responsibility of the spiritual load that came with the position of "pastor." Even if a professor had talked about the subject in seminary, there would have been no way to understand until we experienced it. I could not make sense of all the spiritual and emotional data I was picking up so I needed to talk about it to regain perspective, objectify it, and vent excess emotion. Now I believe that those people who rejected me and actively shut down my expression of emotion were also burden bearers who could not tolerate any more pressure. Their cups were full, and they did not want me to spill mine into theirs. I do not think they understood what they were doing or why they reacted as they did, but it was very hurtful to me. I became reluctant to be open with anyone about anything meaningful for many years.

In later years, as we learned of burden bearing, we found that sharing with a few trusted people meant much less accumulated spiritual debris. Accountability friends help us sort to see what is to be left at the cross, what is to be an ongoing intercession—and as such to be carried in the heart for a time—and what is a cutting edge in our own spiritual and emotional development.

COMMUNICATION AND TRUST

A part of learning to trust others is learning to communicate. You may not communicate what you experience because of past rejections and minimizations. Within the safety of a small group of trusted friends is a good place to start learning to share these experiences. Empathetic connections open up lines of communication and give direction for conversation as well as prayer—points from which to begin asking questions to clarify what you sense. Clarification reveals a person's readiness for conversation or prayer and models healthy openness. When I ask for clarification, I model asking to have my needs met. I want to relate; I need more information. People realize it is OK to have a need, a want.

Granted, the need for clarification may not be as great as other needs, but there is a scriptural principle here—be faithful with a little and more is given. *"Because you have been trustworthy in a very small matter, take charge of ten cities"* (Luke 19:17). When people share a little need, hurt, hope, or want and you faithfully treat their story with respect, they will trust you with more. Respect the story and you respect the person. Respect earns trust, making it safe to express more need and expect that to be met as well. Trusting at this level is foundational. As you model it for others and see others model it for you, you become freer and more able to trust others and God—and ultimately yourself. For some, intimacy is foreign. Although most people would say they want it, they still fear it. Do not be discouraged or alarmed at the amount of time it takes before you feel free to express what is deep in your heart and heavy on your mind.

Unfortunately, many of you grew up in homes in which needs, wants, and emotions were not acceptable. Once you learn that they are acceptable, the Lord may connect you with someone else who needs to learn that needs and wants are normal. The Lord may ask you to demonstrate for someone that you will not belittle or rage at her for making needs and wants known. Use your empathy to sense what direction to ask questions in, what comments will express understanding, and how to show your interest, empathy, and caring. Using empathy in this way probably feels logical and "normal," and it is—it is doing what Jesus would do! God notices and does not forget.

HIGH SENSITIVITY, COMMUNICATION, AND TRUST

Broken trust is probably the deepest cause of communication difficulties. You do not communicate things of the heart if you do not believe those precious things will meet with acceptance and respect. You will not allow intimacy to develop when you do not trust another to cherish who and what you are; rather, you may try to give them what you think they want.

A common difficulty you may experience with communication as a highly sensitive burden bearer is dissonance between the words spoken and what your "insides" tell you. Your spirit may interpret the dissonance as deceit or duplicity, which is problematic when coming from a family member or someone who "loves" you. In that case, it is easier to choose to be confused rather than confront or clarify. This has two effects:

1. You assume you are in error, "It must be me. I must be hearing incorrectly," so you distrust yourself. Dissonance creates confusion and uncertainty. What do you believe, the gut feeling or the words? This is called "crazy-making," which can fuel feelings of low self-esteem and low self worth.

2. Dissonance builds distrust. You may feel lied to, or you may feel like the speaker is trying to hide something, so you do not trust him.

Your high sensitivity can interfere with communication. Ron[2] withheld comments about housekeeping out of respect for Rhonda, his wife. If he said what he thought, he would pay a price. However, withholding created tension in him. Rhonda, being a sensitive wife, felt his tension and was hurt because he would not be open about what was bothering him. She did not want to hurt him or pay the price she might have to pay for "being nosy," so she said nothing. He sensed her hurt, and his burden became even heavier. So the tension in both of them built until one of them exploded. They both said things they did not mean and later regretted. Sensitivity in this case created more heat than light; it fuelled tension rather than diffused it. Mishandling sensitivity blocked intimacy, built distrust, and put a wedge in unity.

On the other hand, high sensitivity can facilitate communication. You can help others clarify and harmonize what they think, feel, and say. Reflecting back to people what you hear, sense, and feel can help them settle confusion and know more surely where they stand and how they feel. High sensitivity can help identify feelings and sort out the individual threads of a ball of emotion.

TRUSTING GOD

Talking to yourself is one way of learning to trust God when it seems like He is doing nothing to lessen earthly pain. The Psalms record King David's inner conversations. *"Why are you so downcast O my soul...?"* (Ps. 42:11). Remind yourself of what you know to be true about God from your own experience, as King David did. Remember what He has said about Himself. Memorize Scriptures about the nature of *God*. It gives you something positive to meditate on—something "to think intently and at length, to reflect deeply on."[3]

Pull up memorized Scripture to chew on in times of doubt or fear. Then make a decision—who are you going to believe? God or the rude Philistines who would have you believe a lie? God gave you a mind; it is a good thing. Use your mind to change your focus. You can choose to look for those things that prove the goodness of God rather than focus on negatives. As you begin to change focus, you will see more and more. It is like buying a Volkswagen—after you own one, you see all the others on the road you never noticed before.

TRUSTING SELF

If you have been minimized, dismissed, and rejected for a lifetime, you may have little to work with when trying to learn to trust yourself. The internal messages that you are stupid, unimportant, and unworthy die slowly.

Remember that foundationally you are a concrete learner regardless of the learning style you adopt later on. All infants need to touch, taste, and feel to develop meaning—in the same way you need to experience trust before it can become a part of you. Keeping company with people who trust God and each other, you can dare to experiment.

I remember watching my roommates in college as they analyzed each other's papers. I saw that it was a critique of the writing, not of the person. Before seeing this separation and if I could prevent it, I never allowed anyone to read anything I wrote except the professor. My experience in school as a child was that criticism of my work was criticizing my person. There was no critique—only criticism. I was delighted to find that my work was not "me," that someone can criticize what I do without rejecting me.

Learning by seeing gave me the courage to learn by doing. Trying to trust gave me the experience of trust—finally I had something to build on. Many people have this same dilemma—they recognize no distinction between what they produce and who they are. Therefore, their only protection from withering criticism is to build a shell. In a small group of people, committed to each other and on the same journey, you can help each other learn trust. You can give each other the feedback you need to learn that what you feel is not who you are. This is a huge learning curve for natural burden bearers.

Don't Relate?

If you are one of the lucky few who feels they do not have trust issues (at least they are not glaring and in your face), praise God! That was my situation. I was given the task of presenting a talk on Basic Trust. I studied and studied, but did not feel right about giving the presentation. Finally, I went to the Lord with my dilemma. "What am I to do, Abba? I cannot relate to this material. How can I present it in a helpful manner? Perhaps the work should be reassigned, yes?"

Gently, the Lord led me to the Scripture. Luke 9:57-62 says,

As they were walking along the road, a man said to Him, "I will follow you wherever you go." Jesus replied, "Foxes have holes and birds of the air have nests, but the Son of Man has no place to lay his head." He said to another man, "Follow me." But the man replied, "Lord, first let me go and bury my father." Jesus said to him, "Let the dead bury their own dead, but you go and proclaim the kingdom of God." Still another said, "I will follow you, Lord; but first let me go back and say good-bye to my family." Jesus replied, "No one who puts his hand to the plow and looks back is fit for service in the kingdom of God."

The bottom line is, wherever you find a "yes, but" or a "but Lord," you have identified a fissure in your trust. It may not be an outright break, but a fissure. It is a point of weakness that results in disobedience or, at best, qualified obedience. Something or someone takes precedent over obedience. The trust is not yet broken, but a blow to that area, too much stress in that area, will break it. The Lord wants to mend the fissures in your trust—to fill you with His love and life so that the fissure is filled from the inside out. He wants to mend you so completely that from the outside there is no evidence that there ever was even a fissure; He wants you to have no scars. He wants your trust in Him and of Him to be completely intact.

ENDNOTES

1. For more on basic trust see John and Paula Sandford, *Transformation of the Inner Man* (South Plainfield, NJ: Victory House Publishers, 1982), 143-168, and E. James Wilder, *The Complete Guide to Living With Men* (Pasadena, CA: Shepherd's House, 2004).

2. Fictional names—the actual names of individuals are always changed to protect privacy. If this is your story and your name, it is purely coincidental!

3. *One Look Dictionary Search,* s.v. "Meditate," http://www.onelook.com/?w=meditate&ls=a (accessed March 3, 2010).

CHAPTER 8

Making and Keeping Boundaries

THIS DISCUSSION OF BOUNDARIES WILL be limited to the need for the particular boundaries essential for burden bearers' spiritual, physical, and mental well-being. Many good resources are available on the subject of boundaries, the impact they have on your life, and the consequences of the lack of them. All of that need not be addressed here.

Boundaries are stopping places. To make stopping places appropriate to you as a burden bearer, begin by identifying your underlying values. Once you create boundaries that reflect your values, you can develop gracious and appropriate ways to hold or defend them. If your family of origin did not teach and practice stopping before offending or violating, the holding, maintenance, and defense of boundaries is a critical lesson. You can find exercises to complete on my Website that will help; it will also give you tools to help others with their boundaries (www.fromGodsheart. com). Without boundaries, you have no guideline for saying "no" or "enough." You may allow others to be emotionally, spiritually, or physically intrusive or abusive, or you may be intrusive or abusive to others.

DEVELOP A PERSONAL BASELINE

A personal baseline identifies what you value, what is important to you spiritually, emotionally, mentally, and physically. In light of that, how do you want to act? Identify some core values in each of these areas and write them down. Discrepancies between what you value and what you allow to happen point to areas in which you may wish to make or amend a boundary. For example, I value a quiet time with God in the morning—alone. We live with my very elderly mother who forgets. She is an early riser and quickly wants company. I have to say, "No, I'm not ready yet!" If I do not defend that boundary, but claim to hold the value of having quiet time, that is a discrepancy. I would need to amend my behavior or admit that I am a peacekeeper and evidently value peace and harmony more than I value the quiet time!

Once you put words to your values, it is much easier to recognize when you are "not acting like yourself" or the self you want to be. You need to determine whether a burden is pressing you to transgress your boundary, whether there is something in you that needs to be addressed, or whether it is a habit of bad behavior that needs to change. Ask the Lord if you are wearing burdens instead of carrying them to the cross. Develop the habit of stopping, praying about, and correcting your behavior or attitude as quickly as possible whenever you notice thoughts or actions different from "who you value being."

For example, my behavior does not reflect my values when I snap at David (or anyone or anything that is nearby). I value a loving character and a gracious tongue; I do not want to act like a shrew. I make an internal boundary for the kind of speech I allow myself. On occasion, a rude Philistine sneaks in and begins to mess with my emotions. I become aware of feeling that "there is a conspiracy to make my life difficult." Before long, those feelings dictate my behavior. Feelings are transient. I do not value feelings pushing me around—that is not the "me" I want to be. I need an internal stopping place for feelings. Awareness brings a choice. I can give myself an attitude adjustment, or I can be pushed around by feelings and trample on others' boundaries as well as my own.

I value being a good friend, but I must keep a boundary as to how many relationships I can maintain in good conscience. I don't have the energy to go, do, and be a "good friend" with many people. Another boundary I must keep is concerning the kind of people with whom I interact. Some conditions, such as depression, have built-in time boundaries for me because of the emotional, and hence, physical drain they cause. I do not have the emotional resources to support someone indefinitely. Short periods are fine, but extended times quickly wear me out, and I need to withdraw for the sake of my health. I will quickly use up my resources in the presence of high-energy people.

Boundaries that reflect the good value you place on God, others, and self result in giving honor and respect. You show your honor and respect of God by honoring the frame He gave you as you learn appropriate boundaries and keep them. Whether you are aware of them or not, your limits—physically, mentally, emotionally, and spiritually—reflect His design.

LEARNING YOUR BOUNDARIES

Studying your values is one way to delineate boundaries, but sometimes you learn where they lie by trial and error. A colleague once wanted me to help her learn to make and hold boundaries. She asked me what mine were. I was unable to think of any when asked directly. However, I made a commitment to be honest with her when she stepped over or on one of them. We both recognized when *that* happened! When the dust cleared, we discovered a wide line in the sand! My honesty helped her begin to learn where I began, and therefore, where she stopped.

Another way to discover hidden boundaries is to make a list of times you have felt hurt, caught in a double bind, violated, or abused. Lay it alongside your list of values; see if you and a friend can find words for the "line" that was crossed. Do you need to change the "line" to match your values? The Lord will help you learn where your limits are, sometimes directly and sometimes with the help of friends. Once you establish your boundaries, you are responsible to maintain them with His help. Your part in your maturity and development is to be responsible for self-management. You will find yourself overburdened and overwhelmed or hurt and feeling violated or taken advantage of when you transgress your boundaries or allow others to do so. God designed you to carry or endure a certain amount in order to do just so much. Going beyond that will result in physical, emotional, and spiritual consequences.

Scooping up burdens without the Lord's direction is one boundary you do not want to cross. You will tire and begin to break down after a time. The very pain and trouble you wish to make better will come between the Lord and you. Unfortunately, many highly sensitive natural burden bearers are the dumping bins for families, workplaces, and churches; burdens seem to stick to you. People throw them your way regardless of size, frequency, or toxicity—most often reflexively, not even knowing they are doing so.

You honor what you value. Boundaries are a way of giving those values substance. If you truly value time with the Lord, your family, the Church family, and self, then that will be reflected in the boundaries you keep and the limits you put on yourself, other people, and activities.

The next step in setting appropriate limits is to learn how much energy you have to spend. You have one pool of energy, but four different ways to draw from that pool. Doing spiritual, emotional, and mental tasks draws upon energy reserves, thereby making less available for physical tasks. Doing many physical tasks makes less energy available for spiritual work. You will have to find a balance that is appropriate for you between the various types of activities you value. Learn the amount and quality of recovery time your body, mind, and spirit need, and make your decisions accordingly. "I can do this and this, but not that." Empathy is a type of work; it requires physical, mental, and emotional energy. Burden bearing, in addition, requires even more energy. You do not normally think of burden bearing as work, but you do expend energy in the burden bearing process. You must learn the effects your activities have upon your spirit, emotions, mind, and body and not spend what you do not have. You may need to alternate types of activity to make room for renewal and refreshment. There is real merit to the old saying, "All work and no play make Jack a dull boy." Lack of variety, as well as over-extension, dulls your sensitivity to God, others, and yourself.

God gave each tribe of Israel specific boundaries when they entered into the Promised Land. They knew precisely where one tribe stopped and another began. They knew their limitations geographically, what they were responsible for (land, festivals, laws, sacrifices, tithe), and what to defend. You need equally specific boundaries to define your limits and responsibilities spiritually, emotionally, and physically. How far can you go? How much can you carry? For what are you responsible? When does someone else's responsibility begin?

God does not ask you to respond to every need that you see; He does not ask you to take on every spiritual battle that you see. He does not ask you to carry *all* the needy people in your life. The Lord wants you to learn your built-in limits as part of your development and maturity. He knows your strengths and energies better than you do and will help if you ask Him. Learning to live within these limits is one way of developing the nature and character of Christ in your life. If you are to be healthy and full of joy, learn the discipline of sending up a flare prayer and walking on past whatever the Lord does not ask you to carry. Jesus modeled this. He walked away from crowds of needy people—it was time to go to the next village (see Mark 1:38). Learn to sit, helpless, with a person in need if you do not have the required resources; this is what Jesus asked of Peter, James, and John in Gethsemane. They could not help Jesus take all the sin of humanity unto Himself, but they could have provided companionship. Give hurting people companionship. Learn to be humble enough and trust God enough to ask Him to fight spiritual battles for you, in your place, and to carry those you love.

Learn the discipline of walking past all the clamoring social needs and all the needy people to the *one* the Lord highlights. You will have to work at this because at the core of most burden bearers is an unspoken belief that "No one else is going to do anything about the trouble in the world, so I had better get busy!" *Just because you see a need does not make you responsible to fix it.* You are responsible to send up a prayer as a flare to mark the spot. You are responsible to ask the Lord to send the one who *is* called to minister, to fix the need, but you are not always responsible to fix it yourself.

On the other hand, if God *is* calling you to bear someone's burden, to come alongside, or even to carry a portion of his troubles in the heart for a time, He will give the grace and strength to do it. The Lord obligates Himself to see a work to completion when He begins it (see Phil. 1:6). When He does not authorize a work, but you pick it up out of reflex, you do so in your own strength not His—you will wear yourself out.

Spiritual Boundaries

Spiritual boundaries are probably the hardest to develop and maintain for the natural burden bearer. You may feel contamination when you absorb a portion of someone's burden that God has not called you to bear. You need to be aware of the toxicity of wrongful burden bearing; factor that in when making decisions about various activities. You need not fear the feeling of contamination that may come with burden bearing; you can turn to Jesus for cleansing. But you must keep in mind the kind of spiritual environment you will be exposing yourself to when assessing your resources. Do not knowingly walk into an environment you are not built for or called to.

For example, do you have the spiritual resources to maintain your balance in the presence of strong religious spirits? Or should you join a group that is doing spiritual warfare to "take the city" for God? People called to work on the "front lines" in spiritual warfare are spiritually equipped to do so. A person called to be *support* for the "front lines" finds spiritual warfare quickly becoming toxic to them. If they stay in that environment too long, they quickly expend their resources and become prey to the enemy.

You can know a thing with your mind, but your heart can still want to operate the old way. It will take time to bring your emotional responses into line with what the Lord has revealed. You may forget to check with the Holy Spirit when someone is in your face asking for help, and thus, you may take on things the Lord is not asking. In time, you will recognize these infractions more quickly and repent of presumption more easily. You will become kinder to yourself and not condemn. You would never expect a child to have an adult vocabulary in one year. Yet we do expect ourselves to discern correctly all the time when we have only recently begun to understand burden bearing. Why do we do that?

Doing a new thing wrong is part of the learning process. Your Heavenly Father is one of those fathers who helps His children up when they fall, helps them regain balance, encourages them to try again, and compliments them for trying at all! It takes time to learn Kingdom language and Kingdom ways.

PHYSICAL BOUNDARIES

Much is written about physical boundaries. I want to call your attention to the particular physical need that burden bearers easily overlook. It has to do with your "sanctum sanctorum"—your place to go for renewal. Jesus went out to a "lonely place" to have renewal time with His father (see Mark 1:35). You also need a physical place to go for renewal. One person may have a specific path for a nature walk, or he may like to go fishing. Another may need a quiet spot in the garden or a room decorated to taste. You need a private place you can retire to for refreshment. Identify your place, create one if you need to, and make boundaries regarding it. Is it off limits to everyone, or can you allow someone in? Determine how much time you need to spend there and how often. As you respect your need for renewal and attend to that need, you have made a boundary.

If you are to live a healthy, joy-filled life, you need to learn to choose activities that accurately reflect an understanding of your frame, how God put you together, and how you work. You will need to learn how many activities you can tolerate before needing time in your sanctuary to recover. If the activity involves other people, how many people can you be with before becoming overwhelmed? With what type of people will you be interacting? What are the circumstances, the environment, and the nature of the activity?

You need to learn whether you are a project person or whether you can tolerate being part of a "never ending" task. For example, I can help with summer Bible School because it has a beginning and an end. I do not do well teaching Sunday school because that goes on forever. I did well as a university instructor because of the built-in time off. Similarly, although I can do administration, the limited time away from the work environment and the never-ending nature of the task does not suit me. If we have a houseguest, that is my activity for the week. David and I factor in a week of recovery time upon return when we travel. Extroverted activities drain my energy; I must balance an extrovert activity with equivalent introvert time to recover.

EMOTIONAL BOUNDARIES

Emotions affect energies, and energies affect emotions. Your brain automatically synchronizes with the people you are with—this draws from your pool of emotional energy. What kind of emotional space are you in? Some days just being present is a huge job for me;

maintaining eye contact and following a conversation is all I can do. How much emotion can you give out before you must "refuel"? The type of person you relate to, what you allow others to put on you or pull out of you, and your inner strength or fragility are all a part.

Do you know when to make someone stop, when to say *"no,"* or that you even have the right to say "no"? If not, you may have been "designated" to do the emotional work for the family; you may have become the dumping ground for others' emotions. Learning to say your *"no"* is how to maintain these emotional boundaries.

Some people want to be self-revelatory and want you to be the same, whether or not that is comfortable for you. They and you must learn where you stop and they begin and to respect that boundary. It becomes very difficult to say "no" if forbidden to do so. At times you are able to cope with relational requests and other times not. Inability to relate may have everything to do with your present energy level or inner fragility rather than being a rejection of the person making the request—communicate these things to diffuse tension. Relating may be more than you can do at present.

An example would be not wanting to take on an ongoing relationship with a deeply depressed person if you are immersed in your own struggle with depression. Sometimes, being aware of history, you may know that a certain person's presence requires resources you do not have. You may feel guilty when someone asks to relate to you, but you cannot. Some people try to make you feel guilty if you do not show any signs of guilt. Guilt trips are too expensive! I don't recommend them!

It helps to have support. As our daughters were learning to say "no" to peer pressure, we made an agreement. If anyone called, asking them to go out, and Meilee or Michelle did not want to go, but didn't quite have the inner strength to say "no" for themselves, they could say, "Mom, can I?" but shake their heads *no!* I would obligingly say, "No, you cannot!" Later I would ask what I had told them they could not do! Having moral support is wisdom, not weakness, when learning to say "no." Neither daughter has trouble saying "no" as an adult!

In *The Mystery of Spiritual Sensitivity*, I told the story of a friend who wanted to relate in a way that felt to me like psychic nudity (telling everything)! In that case, she asked me to relate to her when I had neither the emotional or physical resources, nor the inclination. I knew that the intensity of her desire came out of her own loneliness and wounding, but I sensed that her neediness could easily overwhelm me. If I were overwhelmed, I would be of no use to her as a friend. You actually honor the other person when you honestly admit you are unable to relate. Such a statement is about you, not them.

Some individuals are adept at twisting words to make a "me" statement into a "you" accusation! That is your cue to exit the conversation. You will violate your own boundaries if you stay to try to mend the misunderstanding. You allow others to manipulate you into relating when you have already made it clear that you had no further energy to do so. It is not constructive to continue to argue or correct. Arguing, attempting to clarify or correct, can cause more heat than light—it only uses additional energy. Simply say, "I need to go now." And go.

Another boundary issue surfaces when people want to relate to you so that you will do their emotional work for them. They pick until you cry so they do not have to, they push you to anger to alleviate their tensions, or they wander off and abandon you to relate to a crotchety relative. They try to make you feel guilty if you do not take on their emotional labors and relational responsibilities even though God did not ask you to. An accountability group can be of great help in sorting these things out. Ask for moral support when you need it. Reflexes of a lifetime do not change in a month!

I mentioned high-energy people earlier. Whenever you try to synchronize your emotional state with theirs, reaching their emotional level may drain you. This is not to condemn someone with high energy. Personally, I wish I had the vim and vigor I see in some people, but acknowledge that I do not and move away from such energy spending when I need to. If I do not take the time to disconnect, I spend my little energy quickly and become a wet blanket to the high-energy person. I overextend and am of no good to God, my friends, or myself. Better to give a bit with grace and love than to give nothing at all! Remember that empathy brings your emotional state into sync with another—which may drain you too much if you are not careful.

I have several such high-energy friends. Since multiple sclerosis has dramatically lowered my energy level and limited my ability to develop reserves, I have to keep some distance. I enjoy watching them bounce around, but close proximity quickly fatigues rather than uplifts. Out of respect for the present condition of the frame God made, I have learned to ask them to reign in their emotional energy so that I am not tempted to try to match that high level. We all value the relationship, so I have learned to be honest with them, and they graciously accommodate me.

A similar energy drain happens when burden bearers are near people whose needs are monumental. A description that springs to mind is "train wreck." You do not even have to be talking about their troubles; just being in their presence will do it! I have learned that I must be the best friend I can be for the time I can be and then pray and let God handle the situation. Saying *no,* stepping back, and limiting involvement before crashing is a difficult discipline when your orientation is always to give. However, it is a very necessary discipline if you want to partner with the Lord for the long term.

FUNCTIONING IN A GROUP OF PEOPLE

You can ask the Lord for a special coat of "spiritual insulation" when you know you are going to be with a new group of people. The volume of emotional distress and spiritual toxicity can be so great in a group that you can be overwhelmed and miss what the Lord would have you address. Empathetically, the emotional, spiritual, and physical data from the people around you comes as an undifferentiated mass. It is not much different than standing in a stream with a strong current—it requires strength and endurance to keep your balance. When in a group, you can ask the Lord to cover you from indiscriminate burden bearing and help you find the one He wants you to come alongside—if any. The Lord can highlight an individual so that she stands out and you are drawn only to her. Note when this happens and ask the Lord what is in His heart to do.

DOUBLE BINDS, GUILT, AND BURDEN BEARING

Binds and double binds use fear and guilt to operate; they make keeping boundaries problematic. A "bind" is a situation in which you fear you must do something. You do not have the option of choice. The only choice is conform to pressure or endure punishment. A "double bind" forces you to choose, but you receive punishment or blame regardless of your choices. A classic double bind occurs when a parent assumes a child is guilty and determines to continue spanking, hitting, or lecturing until the child cries. However, the child knows

HIGHLY SENSITIVE

that crying is seen as an admission of guilt. Worse, as soon as the child cries, the authority figure punishes him for crying. "Stop that or I'll give you something to cry about!" The child is bad for not crying, and is bad for crying. In that scenario, multiple boundaries are broken.

Carrie, a highly sensitive burden bearer, had a dream. "I was given a job as a nurse, but had not yet been given an orientation. My assignment was the surgery technical floor, and I was in charge of the other nurses for the night. I was in charge, but did not understand what we were to do. The supervisor came by, and I expressed concern about being in charge of others when it was not clear to me what my own duties were. She said, "Oh, you will understand once you get the orientation." The dream matched patterns of her parents' behavior in her growing up years and of her ex-husband and authority figures as an adult. They gave her responsibility without properly preparing her for it.

Another way of describing a double bind is that you must, but you cannot. You cannot do what is demanded of you, but if you try, you will suffer for it anyway. The following are different facets of the double bind in the dream:

1. There was no admission that Carrie was right to be concerned. No one validated her stress. No one acknowledged that the problem existed.

2. The supervisor avoided admitting that she and the others in charge had done wrong. They had not oriented her before making her responsible. The supervisor was truly guilty, but not admitting it, thus projecting her guilt onto Carrie.

3. Authorities dismissed her concern. She felt no one believed her, and, apparently, her needs were

not important. This left her in a quandary with
no viable answers.

The following are some of the feelings generated by the
double bind of the dream. If Carrie persisted and tried to explain
her concern so that someone would take action to avoid trouble,
she would be condemned for saying "ouch," as though she were
blaming the supervisor. She feared her persistence would be seen
as trying to draw attention to her concern too long after the initial
dismissal. Consequently, she felt that she was wrong and bad. She
felt it was her fault for causing stress by trying to explain that she
was not sure what they wanted her to do. She felt she was bad for
telling the truth that she did not understand. She would only be
accepted and tolerated if she lied, said what they wanted to hear,
and acted as though there was no problem. Yet when the thing she
was concerned about happened, they blamed her for whatever went
wrong. Broken boundaries, boundaries never made, blame, guilt,
and fear abounded! Can anyone relate?

Carrie's prayer partner saw that to some degree she was lost in a
fog of blame. She confirmed that was indeed how she felt. In prayer,
they asked Jesus to bring her out of the fog of blame. They asked
Him to take authority over parents' words of blame that created the
fog, to untangle the blame they had dumped on her and that she
had absorbed by wrongly bearing and wearing the burden of blame
(the supervisor was a symbol of her parents. The Lord wanted her
to see that fact).

Two patterns left her feeling at fault for anything that went wrong.
The first pattern: She absorbed the feelings of guilt others carried for
whatever went wrong. Whatever guilt others put on her, she wore.
She absorbed as much guilt as possible whenever she sensed it in her
parents, valid or otherwise. She had been doing that from day one!

The first pattern: Both parents did have valid guilt for wrong things they did. However, they grew up being blamed for things that were not their fault. Both parents were in a fog of false guilt, from blame for things that did not belong to them. When you are condemned for minor mistakes as well as for actual faults, or just for being there, it is difficult to face those faults and ask forgiveness for anything. You cannot trust that you will receive mercy when condemnation is all you expect and admission of any wrongdoing only makes matters worse. Because Carrie's parents grew up having to be either perfect or worthless, they couldn't or wouldn't admit when they were wrong and their daughter was right. They did to her what they had judged their parents for doing—they blamed everything on the child.

The second pattern: Carrie did to herself what she judged her parents for doing. They dismissed her and refused to believe her. When she thought that someone was wrong and she was right, all too often she dismissed her thoughts with, "What if I'm wrong?" She would not, could not, believe herself. She listened to the rude Philistines and believed the lie that she deserved condemnation and turmoil—not always, but all too often.

You can easily guess what habit Carrie's mother had—continually worrying that she might be wrong. Her daughter sensed and absorbed this feeling and thought pattern and wore it as her own, until truly, it was hers as well. She had not recognized that she learned this habit from her mother because her mother was so blaming and tough on the surface. She remained tough and blaming until a crisis with an older sibling. The crisis changed her mom; she became compliant, repressing thoughts and feelings with only occasional explosions. Of course the mother felt that the crisis with the older sibling was all her fault, that she was a part of his crisis! She did have a part, but only a part. The father was also involved. There were others in relationship with the son (the older sibling), and let's not forget the man's own choices that were a part of his crises.

The family crisis brought these patterns to the forefront. As a result of the prayer ministry during the crisis, Carrie has new boundaries. She is learning not to dismiss her sense of truth. It is now much harder for people to make her wear guilt that is not her own.

If you are guilty for everything and anything, there are no stopping places, no boundaries. You have no way of finding boundaries for yourself when your authority figures had none. You have no reference points from which to build boundaries. Learn how to avoid guilt trips. Determine where you stop and someone else begins and who is actually responsible for what. Learning to make these distinctions is essential for the mental and physical health of all burden bearers. An accountability group can help you develop these kinds of emotional and spiritual boundaries. Jesus is your travel agent; refer all guilt trips to Him!

Appropriate Helplessness

The Lord knows your frame, what is appropriate for you, and He is willing to limit what you see and sense. Only He is God and able to see and bear all things. God is able to redeem your burden bearing capacity when you surrender the management of the gifting to Him. In other words, you put the sensitivity of your human spirit under His control. Abraham fathered Isaac, the son of promise, but God asked him to sacrifice his son, to release his son back to God as an expression of his faith in God. God so honored Abraham's willingness that He not only spared Isaac, but also provided a ram for the sacrifice (see Gen. 22:13). God not only provides good gifts, He is also the provider of all you need. Give the ability of burden bearing back to God. Under management of the Holy Spirit, you will see and hear selectively what God wants you to see and hear.

At times helplessness is appropriate. Allow God to limit you. The Lord limited Gideon's army (see Judg. 6–8). At times, you may see or hear someone's pain, but do not know what to do about it. You may be helpless to do anything because the Lord has not directed you to act. When the Lord does not give specific instructions, the best you can do is to admit how awful the situation is, admit your helplessness, and sit respectfully with the suffering one, waiting for direction. You provide the comfort of companionship when you sit and share their suffering, helpless to do anything, but still having the faith to wait for God to come. You can do this for others when someone has done it for you. You are able to identify and empathize because you too have been helpless to do anything about your own troubles. You too have needed someone to come alongside.

Appropriate Assertiveness

The defense of boundaries is a place for appropriate assertiveness. Find a ground (truth) to stand on when people do not take "no" for an answer. From that ground, you can hurl stones (truths) from Jesus at the rude Philistines who amplify guilt trips. For example, when our children were small, I made the decision to be a stay-at-home mom. I was going to be the one to tuck them in at night, not a babysitter. Some choir members, in an effort to fill the ranks, applied guilt to pressure me into joining. My ground to stand on was, "Their father is called to evening church meetings, but God is not asking me to deprive my children of their mother as well." I did not try to explain or defend myself when they put forward other objections, nor did I try to explain what I saw wrong with their reasoning. I simply repeated myself, "I am called to be with my children." Finally, they realized they would receive no other answer and gave up.

In order to protect "down time," David and I find it helpful to commit to a time for ourselves. Then, when someone calls, we can honestly say, "Sorry, I have a commitment." And we do—to God and ourselves. Some may be offended or consider it to be hairsplitting the truth, but if you have difficulty saying "no," you may need to use whatever helps are available until you find it easy to say your "no." Find a truth, a ground to stand on; then you can resist when people tempt you to cross your boundaries. Hidden behind every such temptation is a sneaky, rude Philistine trying to tempt you to make yourself an easy target.

Your boundary lines will become clear as you learn what you truly value, what your energies are, the kinds of people and tasks that feed you, and those things that drain you. Find balance between work, church work, hospitality, personal time, time with the Lord, and time with family. As you do, you will progressively have a better understanding of your energies and consequently your boundaries.

You honor God by living within boundaries that respect the frame He gave you, not by abusing it. By your actions, you demonstrate your faith that God is on His throne, that God loves you and those you love and relate to, and that His plans for us all are good and not evil. God is very pleased when you resign from being the manager of the universe and savior of the world.

THE SAFETY OF ACCOUNTABILITY

Developing several friends who come to truly know you becomes a protection against unredeemed burden bearing. You hold each other accountable to who you are, and you reflect back to each other when you overstep a stated boundary or take on more than you ought to or carry a burden too long. You call each other back when you are not acting like yourselves, and help each other guard time with the Lord and keep life in balance. You provide a sounding board for each other as you learn to recognize the Lord's voice, as you learn to recognize what is "me" and what is not, and you listen with respect to help each other discern which burdens you are to carry and which are to be simply marked with prayer and left with the knowledge that the Lord will send the one who is to carry it. You encourage each other and pray for each other intelligently and specifically.

LIFESTYLE CHANGES

Human beings are such creatures of habit that, for most, change is hard. However, change you must and change you will. Life is change, constant change, especially the Christian life as you embrace the admonition to "be transformed" into the likeness of Christ. You have two options. You can try to maintain the status quo and stand against the flow of the Lord's work in you, or you can work with Him.

Redemption and transformation are God's domain, but self-maintenance is your domain. If you want to partner with God, you must embrace the hard work of change to bring your life into alignment with His direction. You do this by recognizing your design (how you operate best), by creating conscious boundaries, and by doing the hard work of developing habits and disciplines to maintain, strengthen, and defend that alignment.

You can bring your life into alignment with the Lord by making lifestyle changes for spiritual maintenance such as spiritual disciplines: regular Bible reading, regular prayer (personal and with others), regular journaling,[1] regular relationships with other believers, and regular personal and corporate worship. Worship is very important, one-on-one with God and corporately as a church body.

Overly responsible burden bearers may need to learn to relax and play. You may need to develop a hobby. Learn to alternate activities—add something physical to balance out the spiritual—take long walks, build a bird house, climb a mountain, make a flower bed, pull weeds…you get the picture. Do something different! And, laugh. Have fun. God has a good sense of humor. Blow off steam. Your body needs tension releases and stress releases. Friends are good for healthy venting.

One man told me that he has a regular prayer partner and they meet weekly—when they are in the same city the same week! He will rattle on with his tale of joy or woe; the friend listens to it all, claps a big hand on his shoulder, and says, "Wow! That's incredible, I can't imagine!" Then he launches into prayer. He does not try to fix anything or have answers; He just turns to the One who does. You need to talk things out and have someone listen to vent built-up tensions.

However, friends do not jeopardize each other. You may need to vent, but you also need to be aware of the effect your sharing has on whoever is listening. Prayers of release and spiritual hygiene should follow healthy venting.[2] By spiritual hygiene I mean, as you shower to wash away the dirt and sweat of the day, ask the Lord to "shower" you, to cleanse, renew, and refresh the both of you after a venting session. Make sure you and your friend release to Him *all* the emotions and their effects so that you are "clean" and you do not bring negatively charged emotions into other relationships. Ask the Lord to take the resentment or bitterness that you expressed, and your friend listened to, to heal the raw areas, and to fill you both with His peace.

You may need to make another lifestyle change in relation to your work. Is your work and workplace compatible with the values and boundaries you hold? Or, does it perpetuate unhealthy, dysfunctional patterns? Careful consideration and prayer should come before something as huge as a career change.[3]

A LIFETIME OF LEARNING

The burden bearing learning task is large. Maturation into what has been said thus far about burden bearing, trust, boundaries, and living a new way takes time—a long time. God is gracious and does not rebuke us when we ask for wisdom: *"If any of you lacks wisdom he should ask God who gives generously to all without finding fault, and it will be given to him"* (James 1:5). You will lack wisdom, you will fall short, and you will not fully bear burdens rightly the first time or every time. However, if something is worth doing, it is worth doing wrong—worth trying repeatedly until you get it right! Any time you learn a new thing, it can feel awkward and "wrong," but with practice, it becomes natural and "right." Something worth doing is worth doing wrong or imperfectly *until* you are able to do it right!

The Lord does not become upset with you for not knowing some point about burden bearing, but you will be in trouble with the Lord for not pursuing learning once you have become aware. You will be in trouble for not being obedient to practice what you already know. Most natural burden bearers have spent a lifetime assuming responsibility for everything they see or sense that needs to be done or avoiding responsibility in some area. These reflexes will not change in a day. *"Learn what is pleasing to the Lord"* (Eph. 5:10 NASB).

Each burden bearer, not to mention every Christian, must commit to a lifestyle of learning and discovery. The effort of relationship with God and His people builds the character of Christ into you. I heard a parent tell a soon-to-be college student, "When you earn it, you learn it." This is true in spiritual matters as well. You experience more spiritual development and maturity when you work for something than when you put forth no effort. Just as each of you has to learn to walk and talk, you must also learn for yourself how to recognize His voice and the unique signature that burdens carry when the Lord invites you to partner with Him. You must learn to recognize the voice and presence of God as well as His unique way of communicating with you. These things will vary from person to person because we are all unique individuals. We can help each other identify the tasks of learning and provide essential feedback, but ultimately each of us must develop our own spiritual muscles. Any athlete will confirm that building muscle takes time and practice.

Relationships take time. There is no shortcut. Each person must spend time with Jesus, listening to Him, being with Him. That is the only way you will learn to recognize your Lord.[4] That is the only way you will touch His heart. When you do touch His heart, you can move with Him, speak His words, and call on Him to do the good things that are in His heart to do for His people. Having spent time with Him, having learned to come to Him, you can discharge the burdens of the day while He cleanses and restores you because He *knows* you and you *know* Him.

The stretching, learning, and honoring of boundaries is not comfortable, but it is well worth it. Living within your limits lowers stress, resulting in health for the spirit as well as the body. Coming into balance is the key to staying within the boundaries the Lord reveals to you, and thus, it is the key to keeping the healing you receive. There is nothing quite as winsome as a joyful Christian living life with zest.

ENDNOTES

1. Two excellent authors on spiritual disciplines are Richard Foster and Dallas Willard.

2. Brown, Carol, *The Mystery of Spiritual Sensitivity* (Shippensburg, PA: Destiny Image, 2008), Chapter 12.

3. Barrie Jaeger, Ph.D, *Making Work Work for the Highly Sensitive Person* (New York: McGraw Hill, 2004).

4. Max Lucado, *The Song of the King* (Wheaton,IL: Crossway Books, 1995).

CHAPTER 9

The Issue of Identity

DENTITY, THE QUESTION *"WHO AM I?"* is an issue that every burden bearer I know struggles with to some extent. Identity is difficult to grasp and hold when you have been a chameleon, subconsciously morphing into whoever or whatever the strongest personality around needs. The result is a fluctuating, unstable picture of who you are.

Just like a house, your identity needs a "true" foundation. A house that is a few degrees off plumb at the foundation will be several degrees off at the roofline. The walls of your house will not be straight up and down—the house will lean. They will not be as sturdy or dependable in a storm as straight walls are. Your self-image can also become skewed when you are given a picture of yourself that is not accurate. You believe things about yourself that are not true, which prevents you from living your life with joy and confidence. Life can batter you, and you crumble because you are not as "sturdy" as you might otherwise be.

Perhaps by understanding how you form identity in the first place, you can identify what it is missing or needs repair. Then the next question is, how do you repair a damaged identity?

How Identity Is Formed

There are four aspects to identity that are important to note. The first three are the sense of belonging, the sense of worth, and competency. Competency is used to compensate for a shortfall in either belonging or worth. The *sense* of belonging and the *sense* of worth flow from or are the result of a picture you have of yourself. Belonging and worth are a result of how this picture causes you to feel about yourself. However, the *way* in which this picture is acquired is critical, so I call that the fourth aspect.

Inclusion

The sense or feeling of worth comes from inclusion. A lack of worth comes from exclusion. When you were a child, did you have a part in decision making? Did you have choices? Could you choose the clothing you wore, the friends you played with? Could you choose what you wanted for your birthday dinner? Did you choose the paint for your room? Did you choose your education, or were you told what to do and who you would be? Did someone tell you that you would be an engineer, a doctor, a pilot, a teacher, or that you would never amount to anything? Did people talk to you, over you, or about you as if you were a piece of furniture? Were you included in conversations, plans, outings, adventures, and fun? Were your opinions, needs, and desires ignored? Perhaps no one bothered to ask. Did anyone of significance applaud your accomplishments and attend your events?

The Consistent Meeting of Needs

Messages of belonging come from having your needs met and the spirit in which those needs are met. They do not need to be met with an abundance of things, simply with consistency and love. You can have abundance, but if you are treated as an object rather than a cherished child, your sense of belonging will need repair. Mechanical meeting of needs without loving touch and concern or with inconsistent love and concern builds a very shaky sense of belonging. Sometimes you belong, and sometimes you do not. Your heart wonders, which one is this? You become very adept at reading people and sensing their emotional state moment by moment because your safety and security depend upon an accurate assessment. If your belonging is in question or if the criteria for belonging continually shifts, the likelihood that you will need to compensate for a lack of belonging is much greater.

Meeting your needs with consistency and love communicates that you are valued, that you are cherished, and that you are of great worth. This is the truth about you. The heart craves to be loved and cherished. What a dilemma when the people who should love do not or cannot!

COMPETENCY

Competency is where your natural talents come into play. Talent is something you are born with, and it is dependent upon your "group" only in that they can encourage or discourage, help or hinder you. You develop competency when you are pushed to take appropriate risks; that is how you develop the skills necessary to do the task well. Every person needs to feel good about herself; everyone needs to feel that he has worth and belonging. Having both, it is still possible to not rate very high on the competency scale. You can be a klutz and still have a solid sense of self-esteem. However, if a person is weak on belonging and lacks a sense of worth, competency becomes *very* important. You can use competency to compensate for the shortfall in worth or belonging. Your competency can be a source of nurture to your soul when the need to belong is not being met.

What a person is good at does not seem to matter—just that they are good at something! I felt I was not ready for our daughters becoming teenagers, but they did not consult me! I remembered that I had heard someone advise to make sure your teenager is good at something. It does not matter what. Just put your thumb in his back and make sure he is good at *something*. That would get him through his teen years intact! I quickly forgot who said it, but the advice stayed with me! If a child has a knack with computers, help him be the best tech yet. If it is spelling, music, sports, academics, whatever, help your child be able to say, "I'm the best tennis player, diver, runner, stand-up comic, or whatever it is, in school!" The one who does well is valued and included—she belongs!

Many people short on belonging and worth use their competency to buy belonging and worth. The teen short on worth and belonging, but competent in football, will give his heart and soul to the game. He will play in pain or when he is unwell. The pain or illness pales in contrast to the pain of feeling worthless and not belonging. The adulation from fellow students, the camaraderie of the team, and the "atta boys" from the coach—these things far outweigh any pain or illness he may have. He wears his letter jacket to broadcast his belonging and worth to the team.

You see the same pattern in the corporate world. A worker happily takes an added workload or volunteers to head up committees. He drives himself. The job becomes all consuming—worth and belonging are that important. He takes classes to be a more valuable asset to the company. He may display qualifications, accolades, and certificates in prominent places in the office. It is another way of saying, "See me," "Appreciate me." It is proof to him, and to the world, of worth. Sadly, some sacrifice relationships at home in pursuit of the "atta boy" they never heard as a child. When you depend upon competency to *earn* love and a sense of belonging and worth, you open the door that leads to burnout, disappointment, betrayal, and failure. Feelings of worth and belonging that come from meeting expectations, performing brilliantly, or reading people correctly are fragile at best.

In an e-mail to me, Dr. Wilder, psychologist and teacher, put it this way,

> First is that, for the infant and child, the development is focused on an individual identity and from adult on it is on a group identity. It seems that all aspects of identity only become developed and solid when you see them reflected in the "face" of another. It only really becomes "me" when it is the way that *you* see me.

> The common way to establish identity is by the cumulative history of what I have done. That makes me the sum of what has gone before. Since most of that is malfunction and sin, my identity becomes the sum of my errors to *date—as they are seen by others* and reflected to me.

> When I am seen through the eyes of heaven as who I was meant to be and not what I have done then my *potential* defines my

identity. The second point would be that "belonging" is more a characteristic of identity than a requirement for it (identity).

Group identity refers to those you will consider "my people" for your life. You feel at home with your group, your people. You use them as a reference any time you wonder what it would be like you to do in a particular situation. You will turn to your group whenever life becomes too hard. You will bring home your treasures for them to share. You will want them at every important event in your life.[1]

INDIVIDUAL IDENTITY

First I will discuss the individual identity, then the group identity, and then the way that God sees you.

What you see reflected in the faces of the people you relate to during the formation of your "individual identity" creates a picture of yourself. That picture is confirmed when you see it reflected in the faces of the people in your "group"—it solidifies; it becomes real. "You" *are* what you see in those faces. You are what others say you are!

Your emotional response to the picture others create for you is where the *sense* of "belonging" and the *sense* of "worth" come from. It is a sense or a *feeling* of worth and belonging. God designed the family to show you the truth about yourself and the truth about God. If what you see in the faces around you is, in reality, other people's brokenness and sin, you may not learn the truth about yourself. You may feel that you are broken; you are the sin that you see in that face—awful, disgusting, and worthless. You feel you are what others tell you with their faces, words, and body language. One friend put it this way: "When people treat you like a couch, you begin to feel like a couch. They talk about you, over you, ignore you, abuse you, shove you around, use you, throw you away when they are finished with you, but they never talk to you. You feel like a piece of furniture."

Here is another example of a person emotionally responding to the picture others present. For several years when this man was a child, his two brothers, two and four years older respectively, called him "stupid." "Get out of the way, Stupid. Let me do that." He finally concluded he was indeed stupid and proceeded to do poorly in school, act out, and otherwise cause trouble for himself and others. However, he also received other messages, messages of worth and belonging from other members of his family. These same two brothers would also quickly come to his defense when defense was needed. Consequently, there was doubt about whether or not he really was stupid. He had an unstable, fluctuating picture of himself. When he finished his tour of duty in the army, he registered for college, took a couple courses, and received "As." That was all he needed. He proved to himself and anyone who cared to ask that he was not stupid!

Because of your sensitivity, you may feel so different from other family members that you wonder if you were adopted. Another fellow I know would listen to stories his siblings told and wonder what family raised them—certainly not the one in which he grew up! The family reminisced of wonderful adventures, fun, and laughter, whereas the family my friend was familiar with was much darker. Actually, both pictures of the family were true! The siblings did have wonderful adventures; there was much fun and laughter. There was also much pain in some members. My friend was more highly sensitive than the others; therefore, he felt the unexpressed pain. It colored all his family experiences a darker tone. Being aware of the unexpressed pain, he did not perceive the fun or experience the laughter and adventure.

You also may have felt the unexpressed and unresolved trouble of family members, and it colored your experience of life. Your sensitivity may have made your experience of life in the family much darker and more somber. You may feel you do not belong to this family; you are that different from the others.

Your perception that you are different is not wrong, but your conclusion may be. You may have a very accurate perception of the darker reality within your family. If they are not as sensitive as you, they may have not felt their own troubles as acutely as you! You may be quite accurate when you perceive dark and somber emotion or disgust, contempt, and rejection. That may be exactly what a family member was feeling! However, if you assume that every feeling you have originates from your own being or that you caused them to have disgust, contempt, or rejection toward you, you can arrive at a false conclusion about others, God, and yourself. You may conclude that you are "wrong," that there is something about you that is flawed and undesirable. You withdraw to the fringes of the family and wonder if you really belong here. You question your worth.

However, that is not the ultimate reality that God created you to live in, nor is it God's reality. God's reality is the one He designed you for, and the one in which you want to live. God chooses to look at the potential He designed into you rather than the sum total of all your "malfunctions and sins," as Dr. Wilder said! Perhaps that is why He is so patient! He knows what He built into you and that you are capable of doing and being what He has called you to do and be. He knows you can be the person He designed you to be. God looks at an accurate picture of you. You may be looking at a distorted or false picture of yourself.

GROUP IDENTITY

The individual identity is the picture you have of yourself that you put together from what you saw and may continue to see in the faces around you and the way those faces relate to you and your needs.

> Group identity refers to those you will consider "my people" for your life. You feel at home with your group, your people. You use them as a reference any time you wonder what it would be like you to do in a particular situation. The subconscious thought process goes something like this: "Let's see; Mom, Dad, and Uncle Joe say I always do such and such.... So, in this kind of situation it is like me to... *therefore*, now I'm going to...!" You will turn to your group whenever life becomes too hard. You will bring home your treasures for them to share. You will want them at every important event in your life.[2]

As our daughters experimented with leaving the nest, at some point they both called home and with awed voices related how wonderful it was to know beyond any doubt that they could come home. If where they were and what they were doing was too hard, they could always come home. Always. It broke their hearts to hear the stories of girls who had to make their situation work, regardless of interest or abuse, because there was no home to go to. Parents had made it very clear: "Do not come home!"

So, *what if* your "group" had only negative things to say to you and about you? *What if* every time you brought home a treasure they trashed it? *What if* they ignored or mocked your accomplishments?

What if they laughed at or lectured you when life became too hard and you turned to them for some kind of comfort or solace? *What if* they do not consider your important life events important and do not come? *What if* they said, "Don't come home?" *What if* the people in your group are the very ones you would *never* want to attend something of importance to you? How would you feel? Would you feel you belonged to anyone anywhere? If there is no one to look to and no "home" to go to, then who are you and where do you belong? If your needs are not met, or if they are met without love, or if they were met inconsistently, what does that say about your worth to these people? You have no reference points to look to, no one to tell you how to relate to people outside this "group."

Take some time to think about what you saw reflected in the faces of the people in your life as a child. What did their faces say to you? What were the messages? If the messages were that you are good, you are a delight, you are gifted (at something), "you are mine," then you grow up with a strong identity—knowing who you are. If you saw only disgust and contempt, were used and abused, treated as a piece of furniture, or were not "seen" at all, then you may have grown up believing you should be ignored, used, and abused.

If you did not see worth and delight in the faces around you as a child, you may have come to not expect it as an adult, unless the Lord intervenes. If you never know what response to expect as a child, it is unlikely that you do as an adult. Identity involves all those things you look to that tell you who you are, your reference points. What you see reflected in the faces of your community becomes internalized. Much of what you see reflected in the faces of your group is the sum of your history. You do not think to question the truth or accuracy of that picture; that simply is who you are.

REPAIRING IDENTITY

A counselor aligned with Jesus and faithful to His ways can be a great help in repairing identity. Additionally, there are five things *you* can do to repair your individual identity. 1) Produce a zone of belonging. 2) Take the risk of relationship. 3) Wash your mind, spirit, and emotions with God's word. 4) Through inner healing remove the lies about self that you grew up with as well as roots of bitterness toward those who tempted you to adopt those lies. 5) Find new faces that reflect the truth about you. I am sure there are others, but let's just take these five. There is no order of importance indicated; this is simply a list!

PRODUCE A ZONE OF BELONGING

If you feel you are short on belonging, create some! Going back to Dr. Wilder's e-mail,

> If you have an identity, you produce a belonging zone around you. Damage to identity always reduces that belonging zone. *So, it is more important in the long run to continue to produce belonging than to continue to receive it.*[3]

People who have an identity take risks. They include other people. They meet others' needs and have an expectation that their own needs will be met. They feel valued; they enjoy and value someone who includes them, and they reciprocate. The result is a cycle that generates belonging and worth! When you are unsure of your worth and insecure about your belonging, you tend to be more tentative in relationships. Taking risks did not produce good results in the past; consequently, it is difficult as an adult to reach out to relate now.

The Scripture comes to mind that says, *"'Love the Lord your God with all your heart and with all your soul and with all your strength and with all your mind'; **and 'love your neighbor as yourself'"*** (Luke 10:27). You want to be included; so you do for your neighbor what you would like for yourself. To create a "zone of belonging" around you, include others. Make them feel valued and important. That blesses them; they will reciprocate and include you and meet your needs. It becomes a blessed cycle rather than a vicious cycle!

RISK

Take the risk of relationship. Risk is involved in creating or enlarging your zone of belonging. Take the time and the risk to find a prayer partner, a mentor, a counselor—someone you trust who will speak truth into your life—someone to support you. Keep looking and keep asking God to provide such a person. If you feel insecure in your competency, use developing a competency as a point for taking the risk to relate! Find an individual who can help you develop a skill, and make that your reason for hanging out. You legitimately need to see yourself as competent.

WASH YOUR MIND WITH THE WORD

The third thing you can do to repair is to wash your mind, spirit, and emotions with Scriptures that tell you the truth about who you are. Memorize verses that speak powerfully to you so you have them readily accessible in emergencies! Emergencies will come! At the end of this section is a partial list of characteristics of your identity as seen in Scripture. Read them; see if certain verses speak to you. Washing your mind and inner being with the word of God will change the soil of your inner being.

I grew up on a farm in northeast Iowa. Unlike most of Iowa, which has deep, rich top soil, this part somehow escaped the glacier. It is hills, valleys, and clay soil—a hard farm to work. My mother was a gardener and grew a huge garden with flowers wherever she could find a spot to put them. She found an old rose bush planted next to an ancient, dilapidated log cabin on the back 80 acres built by some Irish settlers ages ago. It was a poor, scraggly thing, but she moved it and replanted it. Every time we did laundry, we threw the wash water on the roses. We never thought a thing about it. That was a good place to throw the wash water! In those days, laundry soaps still contained phosphorous. After a few years of feasting on phosphorous rich water, the roses flourished. It was a rambling rose bush and grew all along our back yard fence, a blaze of yellow blooms each summer.

Your identity needs the same kind of treatment. It needs to feed on truth *until* the soil of your mind and spirit becomes rich and you can "bloom."

Inner Healing

Inner healing is essential and will be ongoing. Tend to the wounds that are causing you problems—which is sort of like removing the stick that is poking your side! However, you do not have to put your life on hold and dig up the entire backyard of your life looking for every "root of bitterness" (see Heb. 12:15) that might possibly be there! Instead, having tended to the raw problem areas, go about your life; as you encounter a wound, anger, resentment, or bitterness, receive healing for it. Don't take the attitude that you must "have it all together" before you can take your place in God's Special Forces. You can serve Him while in process. Embrace burden bearing as a lifestyle, engage the struggle to change, take the risks of relationships, develop the disciplines He assigns you, and deal with the inner healing needs as they present themselves.[4]

FIND NEW FACES

The final thing you can do to repair your identity is much harder, but worth the effort. *Find some new faces to look at!* Not just any face will do. What you see reflected in the new faces needs to align with the picture you see in Scripture. The face must also radiate the message, "I am happy to be with you, regardless of how you feel." If a new face does not align with Scripture or does not appear to be happy to be with you, move on—*and do not feel bad about it!* The Lord's will for you is to bloom, not wilt and fade away. You need to have your deficit of truth about yourself met, which means you need to be included—you need to belong.

You will find some faces that meet these criteria, but for a variety of reasons, may not be able to *consistently* meet your needs. Explore the likelihood of their ability to be consistent. Some people have a workload, family responsibilities, and the like that make it unlikely that they would be able to be consistent. They may be willing, but right now, it would be better for them not to take on another relationship.

It is very important to spend time exploring such issues with an individual who "holds promise." You do not need or want to be in a situation where you expect to be consistently included and applauded, but are not. Another alternative is to negotiate and talk about expectations and come to an agreement ahead of time. Then when something "blows up," you can go back and look at your expectations. If there is a commitment to the relationship and to you, your friendship will survive.

It's scary to think about finding new faces. And it's not so easy to do. It takes some measure of healing and strong support from someone you trust to be able to approach something this important. However, we can do hard and scary things! Philippians 4:13 says *"I can do everything through Him who gives me strength."*

God designed the family to teach you who you are. If what you learned in your family was an untrue or unstable picture of yourself, allow God to create a new "group" who can teach you the truth about yourself. You were wounded in relationships, and lasting healing will also come in relationships.

God wants to scoop you up and envelop you in the kind of hug that hugs your insides as well as your outside—that puts "belonging" in your spirit and emotions. When God holds you, it is an indescribable experience. When Paul tried to find words for his experiences, he said in First Corinthians 2:9, *"No eye has seen, no ear has heard, no mind has conceived what God has prepared for those who love Him."*

Language is inadequate when you try to describe experiences with God. He wants you to be able to come to Him and feel belonging as often as you like. He wants you to "abide" with Him, in Him. He wants you to make your "home" with Him, to make Him your "group." He wants you to make *Him* your permanent abode, not a temporary residence. Yes, you need to see God's truth about you reflected in faces you can physically see, but do not stop there—look higher. Look into Jesus' face, into His eyes. Believe what you see there. It is the *Truth!*

How God Sees You

- *"You are the salt of the earth..."* (Matt. 5:13; see also John 17:22). Salt has a preserving quality. The earth is a better place because you are here. Because of you, this world is not completely rotten!

- *"You are the light of the world..."* (Matt. 5:14). You carry the light and glory of God within you. You are the porch light God left on. People lost in darkness can find their way home to God because of you.

God sees that you have worth and value—you belong. He sees your still unrealized potential. He is committed to you becoming all that He intends you to be.

The appendix contains a list of different descriptions of you, different aspects of you from God's point of view. As you read these verses, mark the ones that seem written just for you. Later, go back and memorize the ones you marked. Tuck them away in your memory so you can think about them at any time. Allow God to show you how He sees you and to bring His picture of you from your head to your spirit and emotions.

Look at the third column—note the aspect of your identity that each verse addresses. Remember from the first part of the chapter that your picture of yourself comes from what you see reflected in the faces of those around you. From that picture comes your *sense* of worth and belonging. Look for how these Scriptures show that you are included; look to see how God meets your needs before you know what they are! Do you think that worth and belonging just might be on God's heart? *Just maybe* He wants you to know that you have value in His sight, that you belong to Him. Notice that there is not one derogatory statement about how God sees you or your worth to Him. He does not belittle your competency or cast doubt on your potential. Of course, He knows about all your failures, sins, and malfunctions, but He chooses not to focus on them! He forgives, and it is done. He is not going to talk about your past mistakes unless something continues to hinder you from becoming the person He designed you to be.

Jesus did all the legal work and has prepared a place for you. The Father stands ready to receive you, to give you a new name, to share His name, and Jesus is ready and willing to share His inheritance. The story of the prodigal son in Luke chapter 15 beautifully illustrates God's heart toward you. He is ready and willing to teach you how to live according to the design He gave you. He is ready and willing to enable you to live this life with joy and peace and to prepare you for life with Him. Now take a good look at your current self-image. Compare that with how God pictures you, a believer, in Scripture. Whose picture are you going to believe?

You cannot forget your sins, failures and foul-ups, but you can follow your heavenly Father's example and choose not to dwell on them! Instead, steadfastly choose to look at God's picture of you. See God's picture reflected in faces that are "happy to be with you." The more you focus on His picture of you, the more you are drawn into alignment and agreement with that picture. Choose to believe that truth, even when it feels "wrong." Endure the discomfort of feeling "wrong" until it feels right. This is spiritual rehabilitation. If you lost your dominant hand, you would have to learn to write "other-handed." At first, it would feel wrong, but if you persevered, it would eventually feel "right." Feed your spirit and mind the truth until the distorted images fade and lose their power.

CONNECTING THE DOTS

Now let's bring this around and connect the dots. What does self-image have to do with learning to live with the "gift" of burden bearing? The high sensitivity that makes you a burden bearer has a great deal to do with how you see yourself. How you see yourself affects how you relate to God, what you believe you are able to do and be for Him.

You were not taught, so you did not know that all you feel does not necessarily originate with you, but for a good portion of your life you thought it did. Therefore, you owned all the emotions you felt. Other people's burdens sat on top of your own issues, exaggerating, amplifying, and intensifying what you felt, which caused you to appear over emotional—over the top. Your behavior appeared to be an excessive response. Or when emotion landed on you "out of the blue," you appeared to be emotionally erratic. Your behavior mystified you as well as others. Others saw you as different or weird, and you believed them. You had no explanation.

How you see yourself affects how you relate to God. For example, if you live in anxiety, you approach God more like a cricket than a son—you hop up and down and in and out of His presence. It is difficult to "be still," to be relaxed in His presence, or to hear what He might say to you. You want to learn how to bear burdens in a way that does not empty your "joy bucket" and cause you to crash and burn. Working on bringing your picture of yourself into alignment with God's picture will eliminate a great deal of stress from your relationship with God. Additionally, how you relate to God will affect your relationships with others. Confidence and a new attitude will spill over.

Address the traumas or hurtful experiences that created the fear or anxiety that are part of the mix of how you see and feel about yourself. Your high sensitivity made whatever negative experience you had cut more deeply and colored how you see God. As a child of God, an heir, how you present yourself to Him is vastly different from a cowering servant with a slave mentality. "Furniture thinking" results in a much different posture than the "apple of God's eye" or "beloved of the Most High!"

How you feel and think about yourself affects how you pray. A son who will inherit has more authority than a servant with a slave mentality. Your self-image affects what you believe you have the right to do or to ask God for. How you see yourself literally changes your relationship to God. However, do not feel you have to be fully healed before you embrace the burden bearing learning curve! Engaging and struggling with the problems and burdens God sends your way will bring to light areas that need His healing touch. You may not find these areas any other way!

I acknowledge, with Paul, that you can want to do one thing and actually do another (see Rom. 7:15). Paul said that living "in Christ" is the goal, but I am not always there (see Rom. 7:24). You cannot always hold firmly to God's picture of you, but that is the goal! The more you practice, the more truth you feed your mind, spirit, and emotions, the stronger you become and the more firmly you grasp who you are in Jesus.

Remember that you are learning, and learning means you have not mastered a skill and will not do it perfectly the first time or every time! Mistakes, goof-ups, and lapses are inherent in the learning process—do not beat yourself up for it! Correct the mistake and learn from it, but do not condemn yourself. Jesus does not condemn you; so do not condemn yourself (see Rom. 8:1). It is difficult to eliminate the habit of speaking poorly of and to yourself. When you do, you are doing to yourself what others did to you—you echo words spoken long ago.

Burden bearing is a global experience; you sense things in your spirit, body, and mind simultaneously. Repair of your identity will happen on all those fronts at the same time. It will not happen overnight. One prayer will not do it, but the spiritual discipline of steadfastly choosing God's view of you will. Create some belonging; take appropriate risks. Wash your spirit, mind, and emotions with God's Word. Find some new faces to look at, and *"Taste and see that God is good"* (Ps. 34:8a).

ENDNOTES

1. Dr. E. James Wilder, E-mail conversation with the author, June, 2008. Dr. Wilder is a psychologist, author, and co-founder of Shepherd's House.

2. Ibid.

3. Italics in this quote do not originate with Dr. Wilder, but were added by the author.

4. For more on inner healing, read John Sandford's book *Transformation of the Inner Man* (South Plainfield, NJ: Victory House Publishers, 1982).

CONCLUSION

The Big Reveal

THE TELEVISION SHOW, "EXTREME MAKEOVER," is a wonderful metaphor for a natural burden bearer's life journey. In the "Home Edition" where they work on houses rather than human bodies, structures that are sound and can be salvaged are gutted and completely redone. They put in new wiring and new plumbing, give it a new floor plan, and—*voilà*—create a new home! Many structures are unsafe, and it would be more expensive and time-consuming to renovate than to build from scratch. Demolition of the old is the first step toward the new. Burden bearers who bear burdens in an unredeemed way build protective structures in their hearts and minds. They double wall the protection around extra sensitive areas and block off some inner places entirely—you would never know they existed!

In the course of embracing burden bearing as a way of life, the Lord will remove homemade structures, bring down dividing walls, and put in new foundations when needed. Home Edition workers open up a floor plan to give easy access and put in new windows for air and light. Working with Jesus will restructure you and open you up to a depth of relationship with Him you did not know you could have. You will learn to use your "easy access" to Abba God. He will shed light when you ask.

Jesus had pretty well figured out the blueprint for His life by the time He was 12. He knew what God wanted Him to do with His life and what the outcome would be. But He waited. He waited 18 years—until He was 30! During those years of waiting, He learned and developed (see Luke 2:51-52). It would be good for you to have an idea of where God wants you to go and what He plans for you to do with your life through the design of high sensitivity. What is your blueprint? I believe we can put some of the pieces together like a puzzle and have an approximation of what that might look like!

The first puzzle piece is Galatians 6:2: *"Carry each other's burdens, and in this way you will fulfill the law of Christ."* You find the law of Christ in John 15:17: *"This is My command: Love each other as I have loved you."* First John 3:16 tells us, *"This is how we know what love is: Jesus Christ laid down His life for us. And we ought to lay down our lives for our brothers."* It sounds like "carry each other's burdens" is a part of loving each other!

The phrase, *"carry each other's burdens"* is grammatically inclusive language and is in the command form. It is not an option for more than one reason. First, everyone can do it because everyone has the equipment. That equipment works whether you like it or not, believe it or not. It is not designed to be shut off. Stifling sensitivity is hurtful; it causes damage in one way or another. Second, if you are serious about wanting to follow Christ and fulfill the law of love, bearing burdens is how to do it!

Look at the word *burden* (*baray* in the Greek) in Galatians 6:2. The primary characteristic of this burden is that it is an overwhelming, crushing load. Everyone has experienced such a burden or will at some point in their life. The enemy of your soul conspires to throw one major blow after another at you so that you forget what you know about God and turn away from Him and your design. You "don't want to be so sensitive!" Before you can recover from one blow, another arrives. You begin to understand Job!

The Lord will call a burden bearer to come alongside to help absorb enough of this kind of burden to restore you to yourself and clarify your thinking so that you can make godly decisions, so that you can remember who you are and who God is, and so that you can pray your own prayers. The overwhelming, crushing load takes away your ability to think clearly—you simply try to survive! You become so tired and overwhelmed that you forget to pray. You forget to ask others to pray for you. You forget who you are in Christ. You forget the nature of God and are tempted to become angry or bitter at Him, as if He caused the problem. These times try your faith.

Galatians 6:5 uses a different Greek word for burden— *phortion,* which is more like a soldier's knap sack—it contains all you will need to accomplish your mission. The burden, or load, is appropriate to the vessel carrying it. These burdens (*phortion*) that you are to bear yourself are the difficulties of life that lead to normal human development and maturity. Combined with the discipline of learning to come alongside those under the *baray* in the way Jesus did, they result in physical, emotional, and spiritual development and maturity.

This is the training you need so that upon your "big reveal" you will walk, talk, live, and love as Jesus does. These are the burdens, or problems, that *God allows* in your life, each one designed to bring out something more of Christ that is in you. You find within yourself resources that you did not know were there to solve these problems! Life problems are like the various exercises an athlete practices day after day to build up stamina or develop a particular muscle group. Highly sensitive natural burden bearers often experience their sensitivity as one of life's problems. That very sensitivity is a vital part of the training you need to develop and mature so you can "do Jesus proud" when He presents you to the King!

FULLY EQUIPPED FOR GOOD WORKS

The second puzzle piece is Ephesians 2:10: *"For we are God's workmanship, created in Christ Jesus to do good works, which God prepared in advance for us to do."* Piece number three is your human spirit and physical body. *"I praise You because I am fearfully and wonderfully made; Your works are wonderful, I know that full well"* (Ps. 139:14). Just how wonderfully made are you? The human spirit and body are built to be corporate (i.e., one of the many making up the One Body of Christ). The spirit and body working together have the ability to sense another person's inner state, be that spiritual, *emotional*, or physical. You have the capacity to be able to help carry a portion of what is overwhelming another to the cross. You can carry it on any level, physically, mentally, emotionally, or spiritually. This ability is built into you. Your spirit does it automatically, intuitively; it is time to bring the process into consciousness and develop the reflex of turning to Jesus with burdens.

When others try to make you shut down your sensitivity or when you resist or turn away from your design, there are consequences. First, it hurts when people you care about consider you "unacceptable." Second, turning from God's perfect design for you damages your relationship with Him. God gives you a gift and calls it good, very good, and when you turn away from it, you basically tell Him, "No thanks!" The third consequence for not learning how to work with your design is stunted spiritual development and lack of fulfillment. In an effort to reduce trouble and pain, you give up the amazing life and relationship with God that you are built to have! You do not do the good works God planned in advance for you to do. In this scenario everyone loses—God, others, and you.

However, God did not bring you into the world, stand tall and grand, point to the horizon and say, "Now, go and make me proud," while you stood there distraught because you did not have a clue about what He wanted you to do, how to go about it, or where in the world He was pointing! He does give clues; you just need to know where to look and how to recognize them. He does equip you with all you need to accomplish those good works and make Him proud.

- The first piece of equipment is your highly sensitive central nervous system that sometimes brings you more data than you know what to do with.

- The second piece of equipment is your cingulate cortex, which allows you to synchronize—not only with other people, but also with the heart of God.

- The third piece is your salvation—and Jesus, your coach, companion, and intercessor who continues to intercede for you (see Rom. 8:34). He is the one who loves you as you are, but so much that He is unwilling to let you remain as you are! The love relationship with Jesus keeps developing higher, deeper, wider, and so on. When you truly love, you can accomplish amazing things and put up with or *"bear all things"* (1 Cor. 13:7 NASB)—even the inconvenience that comes from lost sleep because the Lord woke you in the middle of the night to bring someone's sin or trouble to the Cross. Second Corinthians 4:8-11 says it well:

We are hard pressed on every side, but not crushed; perplexed, but not in despair; persecuted, but not abandoned; struck down, but not destroyed. We always carry around in our body the death of Jesus, so that the life of Jesus may also be revealed in our body. For we who are alive are always being given over to death for Jesus' sake, so that His life may be revealed in our mortal body.

- You willingly lay aside the sweetness of being with Jesus, which is your life. You put your comfort aside and take on the "inconvenience" of someone else's sin or distress as Jesus did for you (see 1 John 3:16).

- The fourth piece is the Holy Spirit within you to help make on-the-spot course corrections. The Holy Spirit is your "clue department." Having the Holy Spirit is like having your own inner Garmen, a little GPS device that talks to you! Like the Garmen, the Holy Spirit does not condemn you, yell at you, arch His eyebrows and give you "the look," or call you names when you make a mistake. Rather, He lets you know when you are off course and what to do to regain your course; He tells you when to address burdens and when to put out a flare and continue walking.

- The fifth piece of equipment, when it works as it was designed, is the family—your family of origin and your spiritual family. They are to complement each other, but when one family fails, the other is to pick up the slack.

TRAINING

The fourth puzzle piece is Proverbs 22:6: *"Train a child in the way he should go, and when he is old he will not turn from it."* This verse would be better rendered from the Hebrew as "Train up a child *according to him*, or *in the way of him*, and when he is old he will be true to himself." Highly sensitive people's bodies are designed for burden bearing. Your entire body is an instrument of prayer! The response of turning to Jesus with burdens must become a reflex, acquired with training. You need to train yourself to bear burdens as Jesus did, cleanly. The Holy Spirit within finds the burdens and lifts them up and out of you so that you are not weighed down with residue. When you learn how to live according to your design, you can be true to yourself when you are old. If you never learn, how can you remain true? For highly sensitive people, burden bearing will be one of the *primary ways* God uses to work the nature and character of Jesus into you.

In that light, look at Colossians 1:24: *"Now I rejoice in what was suffered for you, and **I fill up in my flesh what is still lacking** *in regard to Christ's afflictions, for the sake of His body, which is the church.*" Jesus fully paid the price to make reconciliation possible, but did not finish reconciling every human being to God. Many people living today are not reconciled to God, others, or even themselves. As you join Jesus in this ministry of reconciliation, you will find the good works designed for you. He will assign burdens that stretch, challenge, and build your capacities. This ministry is your "spiritual fitness training," your "body building."

Yes, it directly benefits others, but in the process you mature and develop spiritually so that Jesus will be able to proudly present you to the King as a co-heir! Romans 8:17 says, *"Now if we are children, then we are heirs—heirs of God and co-heirs with Christ, if indeed we share in His sufferings in order that we may also share in His glory."* We must first learn how to live as Christ did, to conduct ourselves in a similar manner. Jesus was and is the ultimate burden bearer. He does not ask you and me to bear the quality and quantity of burdens that He bore. He asks us to bear a part, to join Him in the "fellowship of His suffering," not only for how bearing burdens benefits others, but also for our own benefit.

For those of us who are highly sensitive natural burden bearers, burden bearing, or the ministry of reconciliation, is a major tool to help *"Train a child in the way he should go, and when he is old he will not turn from it"* (see Prov. 22:6). Burden bearing is "our way." Regardless of other natural talents that lead you into a certain business, craft, or profession, you need to be trained to build in the reflex that turns immediately to God with burdens. Burden bearing is the way you should go because that is who you are. If you and I are not trained to live our lives according to the design God built into us, how then can we be true to ourselves? How can we ever know fulfillment?

THE BIG REVEAL

You are a co-heir with Jesus! Ideally, heirs receive training to be able to administrate the estate they will inherit. Your inheritance is beyond comprehension, and this life is your training. You are learning to conduct yourself as a son or daughter of a King. This life is your time of preparation. Remember the story of Queen Esther in the Bible book by the same name? Esther had to learn how to walk, talk, and dress like a queen—even how to smell like a queen! She had a year to transform herself from country kid to royal queen (see Esther 2:12). One day Jesus will present you to the King. It will be your "big reveal!" You have one lifetime to learn to walk like Jesus, talk like Him, live like Him, and love like Him.

Romans 8:19 says, *"The creation waits in eager expectation for the sons of God to be revealed."* Usually when you think of "creation," you think of the world and all things in it, but what about Heaven? Heaven is populated by countless created beings, strange and wonderful beyond description! There are rulers, elders, seraphim, cherubim, and spiritual beings such as the wheels with eyes all around that Ezekiel saw (see Ezek. 1:15-18), not to mention the ranks upon ranks of angels of all sorts and description! Perhaps all of this creation also waits—natural and spiritual—on tiptoe, with baited breath, to see the sons and daughters of God.

On that day, as all creation holds its breath, Jesus ushers in the sons and daughters. One by one, He presents us to the King. Abba God looks deeply, lovingly into the face of each man and woman. No one else knows what is communicated in that moment, for no one else can hear what transpires between them. Abba embraces the one standing before Him and says, "Well done. Well done." Then He stands, with an arm around him or her as a very "fit" looking angel takes his place beside the two. With a clarion voice the angel says, "I have been asked to recall for you two or three of the more memorable and inspiring times of overcoming, endurance, and perseverance I had with "so and so" during his lifetime." I realize this angel is a guardian! He is fit because of all the heavy lifting he did during the lifetime of his charge! I could not help but be impressed.

After some time, several individuals have been thus presented, toasted, and applauded. I stand on the edge of the throng closest to the host of heavenly beings and overhear a couple of angels talking. The first angel in the front row notices a small scribe angel sitting at the side of the platform taking down every word. He leans on his friend and lets him know that they would be able to go to the library and view the stories again at leisure! The second comments, "We are able to be in Abba's presence continually, but they cannot see anything more than glimpses of God Almighty, yet they choose Him. How amazing! They cling to Him and, with some ups-and-downs and a few detours, they still keep moving toward the Almighty." It is obvious he feels a deep respect for these human creatures. And so it continues, each son and daughter is introduced, congratulated, and honored. How long it takes, who knows? There are so many—the stories are so riveting! I remember that time is not the same in Heaven.

The sons and daughters of God stand tall and confident; they cannot do otherwise because God has eliminated condemnation. There is no shame or guilt—nothing for which to chide, no regret! No one fidgets or is nervous. Everyone is calm; no one appears to be plagued with the common social ills—shyness, nervousness, and so forth. They know who they are and are comfortable in their skin. Everyone is robed in righteousness and filled with the light and life of God—handsome, beautiful, royalty. Each one is better than the best they have ever been.

My brother-in-law's spinster aunt died some years ago, and I attended the funeral. Mark has several brothers. No one needed to ask which ones were his brothers. They all stood six feet tall, with black, or what used to be black, hair and a similar jaw line. They had a similar walk and personal presentation. The timbre of voice was similar. The family resemblance was strong; each one distinct and individual, but without a doubt, his brother! Similarly, neither will there be any doubt about the sons and daughters of God.

After the last child of God has been presented, Abba God proudly beams at the assembled throng. With delight He points out the strong family resemblance, how each one looks strikingly like Jesus. Then, in a voice that rattles the foundations of the world, He thunders, "Let's hear it for my Son! Let's hear it for *all* my sons and daughters!"

Pandemonium breaks loose. The Four Winds finally exhale with a mighty "whoosh." Thunder claps and Lightening streaks the sky in appreciative applause! A liberated roar of joy rises from the deep. The oceans belly-slam the shores. Mountains rumble, trees clap, and every creature, physical and spiritual, raises its voice in "Hallelujah! Praise God! Holy, Holy, Holy, Lord God Almighty! Magnificent and marvelous are your ways!" You hear shouts, whistles, and stomping. I marvel—all that noise and commotion, but my ears are OK! I have no desire to escape to the parking lot because of the decibels! I am not overwhelmed—not by anything!

The sons and daughters of God stand, receiving the appreciative applause and homage with bemused grins on their faces. As I said, there is no guilt, shame, regret, or condemnation! What else could we do but stand there and grin? At some unseen signal the shouting stops and the music begins. Angels and spiritual beings who have been sitting spellbound for far too long break into dance. Orchestral music comes from somewhere. Massive choirs of angels begin to sing. In jubilation, some angels make loop-de-loops and barrel rolls overhead while others zip back and forth! Creation no longer must contain itself! Joy is the only emotion I can identify—pure, unadulterated joy! It is party time in Heaven!

Abba God begins to herd His sons and daughters off to the right. As we meander, chatting amongst ourselves, I begin to smell the most intriguing, mouth-watering aromas I have yet to encounter. I can tell that my nose has its work cut out for it! It will take a while to isolate, label, and catalogue each aroma with its individual spice or food or combination thereof! Not only are the food smells "out of this world," so is the air itself!

The air reminds me of our first spring in Coeur d'Alene, Idaho. For the entire month of May, the air was warm, clean, and fragrant. The breeze brought whiffs of an intoxicating fragrance that I could not identify or resist. I could not get enough of that smell—I nearly hyperventilated! Later someone told me that it was syringa, a wild shrub of the lilac family—so sweet, pungent, clean, and refreshing! The air in Heaven is like that, life giving and exhilarating.

Light is different too. It does not hurt my eyes. It is brilliant without endangering my retina! My vision is not obstructed in any way. I can see the air and yet see through the air! Each molecule glows, emitting its own light. Fascinating! Is the air alive?! We continue toward the feast, and that is when I notice the gowns. The first thing that strikes me is the variety of color. The heavenly palette has so much more depth to it than ours! My back happily reports the good news that this gown has no label with which to poke me! Then I notice the fabric. I have never seen fabric like this—and I have handled more than a few yards of fabric! It feels *wonderful* on the skin! It flows like nothing I have seen or felt. It swishes, rustles, and ripples. It almost talks to you as you walk, as if it too were alive. I make a mental note: after the banquet, I must ask to talk with the folks in the wardrobe department! I smile, remembering that I said that I wanted to be part of God's Royal Tailoring staff for the first 1,000 years! I wonder how you work with this stuff!

The next thing I notice is the beadwork—no, those are gems all over the bodices of the ladies' gowns. I look closely at my own gown and identify pearls, jade, rubies, diamonds, and sapphires. I wonder what it means; it must have a meaning! The men have gem work on their lapels as well—maybe it signifies rank or division—like the Trident of the Navy Seals, the Wings of the Air Force, or the Anchor of the Coast Guard.

I know this peek into Heaven must close because we are not there yet. This book too must close. I believe God gave me this word picture to paint for you; it is for you to keep. When you are in the trenches, all dirty, sweaty, and mucking about in other people's burdens, not feeling very glorious or victorious, you can remind yourself. Your "big reveal," your graduation party, is just a *part* of the joy set before you! Bring that joy to mind and draw the strength you need to wrestle with your bag of burdens and to hang onto Jesus for as long as it takes! Remind yourself that what you are currently laboring under may be part of the "good works" God designed for you to do from the beginning. Remind yourself that "this labor too will pass, but eternity will not!" He knows how each problem, each struggle molds and shapes you.

I encourage you to embrace your training, your "extreme makeover." Look to Jesus, the author and finisher of your faith. He is the "original" after whom you are being molded and sculpted. As your spirit touches the heart of God and comes into sync with Him, you sense His love and desires for His people. He shares His heart with you so that you carry His life, passion, compassion, love, and healing. You pray, inviting Him into the particular set of burdens and troubles He asks you to bear. As you let God's heart lead you, you begin to look and sound like Him. You begin to be who God designed you to be—a chip off the old block!

It would be wonderful to meet you one day along this journey, have coffee, and share glory stories. If that happens, we can rejoice; if not, I know that one day, at our big reveal, we will meet. Until then,

Abba God, I ask You to be close to my sister, my brother. May Your Holy Spirit be very present, whispering when to turn to the right or the left, when to keep going and when to rest. I ask You to wash over, around, and through them, and that Your Holy Spirit would find every bit of every burden that was not theirs to carry and lift it up and out of them, putting it on the cross of Jesus. Thank you for His effective work on that cross. Comfort and sing over our spirits as we rest in You.

Blessings,
Carol

APPENDIX

You in Scripture

How God Sees You	Scripture	Aspect of Identity
ABLE **M**INISTER	*He has made us competent as ministers of a new covenant* (2 Cor. 3:6a).	Worth and Belonging
ACCEPTED	*He chose us…in Him to the praise of the glory of His grace, by which He made us accepted in the Beloved* (Eph. 1:4, 6.)	Belonging
ADOPTED	*That we might receive the adoption as sons* (Gal. 4:5).	Worth and Belonging
ALIVE IN **C**HRIST	*In Christ all will be made alive* (I Cor. 15:22b).	Worth and Belonging

How God Sees You	Scripture	Aspect of Identity
AMBASSADOR	We are therefore Christ's ambassadors as though GOD were making his appeal through us. We implore you on Christ's behalf: be reconciled to GOD (II Cor. 5:20).	Worth and Belonging
APPLE OF HIS EYE	Keep me as the apple of your eye; hide me under the shadow of your wings (Psalm 17:8). ...He has sent me against the nations which plunder you; for he who touches you, touches the apple of His eye (Zech. 2:8 NASB).	Worth and Belonging
APPRECIATED	God is not unjust; He will not forget your work and the love you have shown Him as you have helped His people and continue to help them (Heb. 6:10). And if anyone gives even a cup of cold water to one of these little ones because he is My disciple, I tell you the truth, he will certainly not lose his reward (Matt. 10:42).	Worth and Belonging

How God Sees You	Scripture	Aspect of Identity
BEAUTIFUL	*You are beautiful, My darling, as Tirzah, lovely as Jerusalem, majestic as troops with banners* (Song of Sol. 6:4). *He has made everything beautiful in its time. He has also set eternity in the hearts of men; yet they cannot fathom what God has done from beginning to end* (Eccles. 3:11).	Worth and Belonging
BELONGS TO GOD	*And you also were included in Christ when you heard the word of truth, the gospel of your salvation. Having believed, you were marked in Him with a seal, the promised Holy Spirit, who is a deposit guaranteeing our inheritance until the redemption of those who are God's possession—to the praise of His glory are God's possession—to the praise of His glory* (Eph. 1:13-14).	Worth and Belonging

How God Sees You	Scripture	Aspect of Identity
BELOVED	As He says in Hosea: "I will call them 'My people' who are not My people; and I will call her 'My loved one' who is not My loved one" (Rom. 9:25). Therefore, as God's chosen people, holy and dearly loved, clothe yourselves with compassion, kindness, humility, gentleness and patience (Col. 3:12).	Worth and Belonging
BLAMELESS	To present her to Himself as a radiant church, without stain or wrinkle or any other blemish, but holy and blameless (Eph. 5:27).	Worth and Belonging
BLESSED	Praise be to the God and Father of our Lord Jesus Christ, who has blessed us in the heavenly realms with every spiritual blessing in Christ (Eph. 1:3).	Worth and Belonging
BRIDE OF THE KING	Then I heard what sounded like a great multitude, like the roar of rushing waters and like loud peals of thunder, shouting: "Hallelujah! For our Lord	Worth and Belonging

How God Sees You	Scripture	Aspect of Identity
BRIDE OF THE KING **(CONT.)**	*God Almighty reigns. Let us rejoice and be glad and give Him glory! For the wedding of the Lamb has come, and His bride has made herself ready. Fine linen, bright and clean, was given her to wear."* [Fine linen stands for the righteous acts of the saints] (Rev. 19:6-8).	Worth and Belonging
	"Do not be afraid; you will not suffer shame. Do not fear disgrace; you will not be humiliated. You will forget the shame of your youth and remember no more the reproach of your widowhood. For your maker is your husband—the Lord Almighty is His name... (Isa. 54:4-5).	Worth and Belonging
	...I promised you to one husband, to Christ... (2 Cor. 11:2).	Belonging
CALLED BY NAME	Fear not, for I have redeemed you; I have summoned you by name; you are Mine (Isa. 43:1b).	Worth and Belonging

How God Sees You	Scripture	Aspect of Identity
CARED FOR	*The Lord is good, a refuge in times of trouble. He cares for those who trust in Him* (Nah. 1:7).	Worth and Belonging
	Cast all your anxiety on Him because He cares for you (1 Pet. 5:7).	Belonging
CHILD OF GOD	*The Spirit Himself testifies with our spirit that we are God's children* (Rom. 8:16).	Worth and Belonging
	Yet to all who received Him, to those who believed in His name, He gave the right to become children of God (John 1:12).	Belonging
CHOSEN	*But you are a chosen people* (1 Pet.2:9a).).	Worth and Belonging
	Therefore, as God's chosen people, holy and dearly loved, clothe yourselves with compassion, kindness, humility, gentleness and patience. (Col. 3:12)	
CLEAN	*You are already clean because of the word I have spoken to you* (John 15:3).	Worth and Belonging

How God Sees You	Scripture	Aspect of Identity
CLOTHED IN RIGHTEOUSNESS	I delight greatly in the Lord; my soul rejoices in my God. For He has clothed me with garments of salvation and arrayed me in a robe of righteousness, as a bridegroom adorns his head like a priest, and as a bride adorns herself with her jewels (Isa. 61:10).	Worth and Belonging
COMPLETE	And you have been given fullness in Christ, who is the head over every power and authority (Col. 2:10).	Worth and Belonging
CONFIDENT	Dear friends, if our hearts do not condemn us, we have confidence before God (1 John 3:21).	Worth and Belonging
CONQUEROR	No, in all these things we are more than conquerors through Him who loved us (Rom. 8:37).	Worth and Belonging
COVERED	I have put My words in your mouth and covered you with the shadow of My hand—I who set the heavens in place, who laid the foundations of the earth, and who say to Zion, "You are My people" (Isa. 51:16).	Worth and Belonging

How God Sees You	Scripture	Aspect of Identity
SON, DAUGHTER OF GOD	*"I will be a Father to you, and you will be My sons and daughters," says the Lord Almighty* (2 Cor. 6:18). *Those who are led by the Spirit of God are sons of God* (Rom. 8:14) *How great is the love the Father has lavished on us, that we should be called children of God! And that is what we are! The reason the world does not know us is that it did not know Him* (1 John 3:1).	Worth and Belonging
DEARLY BELOVED	*Therefore, as God's chosen people, holy and dearly loved, clothe yourselves with compassion, kindness, humility, gentleness and patience.* (Col. 3:12)	Worth and Belonging
DELIGHTFUL	*He brought me out into a spacious place; He rescued me because He delighted in me* (Ps. 18:19).	Worth and Belonging
EXCELLENT	*As for the saints who are in the land, they are the glorious* [KJV: excellent] *ones in whom is all My delight* (Ps. 16:3).	Worth and Belonging

How God Sees You	Scripture	Aspect of Identity
FAITHFUL	*They will make war against the Lamb, but the Lamb will overcome them because He is Lord of lords and King of kings—and with Him will be His called, chosen and faithful followers* (Rev. 17:14) . *I thank Christ Jesus our Lord, who has given me strength, that He considered me faithful, appointing me to His service. Even though I was once a blasphemer and a persecutor and a violent man, I was shown mercy because I acted in ignorance and unbelief* (1 Tim. 1:12-13).	Worth and Belonging
FAVORED	*It was not by their sword that they won the land, nor did their arm bring them victory; it was Your right hand, Your arm, and the light of Your face, for You loved them* [NASB: favored them] (Ps. 44:3).	Worth and Belonging
FEARFULLY AND WONDERFULLY MADE	*I will praise You because I am fearfully and wonderfully made; Your works are wonderful, I know that full well* (Ps. 139:14).	Worth and Belonging

How God Sees You	Scripture	Aspect of Identity
FORGIVEN	*I write to you, dear children, because your sins have been forgiven on account of His name* (1 John 2:12).	Worth and Belonging
FRAGRANCE OF CHRIST	*For we are to God the aroma of Christ among those who are being saved and those who are perishing* (2 Cor. 2:15).	Worth and Belonging
FREE	*Therefore, there is now no condemnation for those who are in Christ Jesus, because through Christ Jesus the law of the Spirit of life set me free from the law of sin and death* (Rom. 8:1-2). *It is for freedom that Christ has set us free. Stand firm, then, and do not let yourselves be burdened again by a yoke of slavery* (Gal. 5:1). *...The truth will set you free* (John 8:32).	Worth and Belonging
FREE OF SHAME	*Do not be afraid; you will not suffer shame. Do not fear disgrace; you will not be humiliated. You will forget the shame of your youth and remember no more the reproach of your widowhood* (Isa. 54:4).	Worth and Belonging

How God Sees You	Scripture	Aspect of Identity
FRIEND OF JESUS	I no longer call you servants, because a servant does not know his master's business. Instead, I have called you friends, for everything that I learned from My Father I have made known to you (John 15:15).	Worth and Belonging
FULLY KNOWN	I am the good shepherd; I know My sheep and My sheep know Me (John 10:14). Now we see but a poor reflection as in a mirror; then we shall see face to face. Now I know in part; then I shall know fully, even as I am fully known (1 Cor. 13:12).	Worth and Belonging
GIFTED	We have different gifts, according to the grace given us. If a man's gift is prophesying, let him use it in proportion to his faith (Rom. 12:6). Each one should use whatever gift he has received to serve others, faithfully administering God's grace in its various forms (1 Pet. 4:10).	Worth and Belonging

How God Sees You	Scripture	Aspect of Identity
GOOD	God saw all that He had made, and it was very good. And there was evening, and there was morning—the sixth day (Gen. 1:31).	Worth and Belonging
HEALED	O Lord my God, I called to You for help and You healed me (Ps. 30:2). But He was pierced for our transgressions, He was crushed for our iniquities; the punishment that brought us peace was upon Him, and by His wounds we are healed (Isa. 53:5).	Worth and Belonging
HEARD	The eyes of the Lord are on the righteous and His ears are attentive to their cry (Ps. 34:15). Then those who feared the Lord talked with each other, and the Lord listened and heard. A scroll of remembrance was written in His presence concerning those who feared the Lord and honored His name (Mal. 3:16).	Worth and Belonging

How God Sees You	Scripture	Aspect of Identity
HEIR	*Now if we are children, then we are heirs—heirs of God and co-heirs with Christ* (Rom. 8:17a).	Worth and Belonging
HIDDEN IN GOD	*For you died, and your life is now hidden with Christ in God* (Col. 3:3). *How great is Your goodness, which You have stored up for those who fear You, which You bestow in the sight of men on those who take refuge in You. In the shelter of Your presence You hide them from the intrigues of men; in Your dwelling You keep them safe from accusing tongues* (Ps. 31:19-20).	Worth and Belonging
HIS JEWEL	*"They will be mine," says the Lord Almighty, "in the day when I make up My treasured possession"* [KJV: jewels] (Mal. 3:17a).	Worth and Belonging
HOLY	*But you are a chosen people, a royal priesthood, a holy nation, a people belonging to God, that you may declare the praises of Him who called you out of darkness into His wonderful light* (1 Pet. 2:9).	Worth and Belonging

How God Sees You	Scripture	Aspect of Identity
HOLY (CONT.)	But now He has reconciled you by Christ's physical body through death to present you holy in His sight, without blemish and free from accusation (Col. 1:22).	Belonging
HONORED	Since you are precious and honored in My sight (Isa. 43:4a).	Worth and Belonging
INVITED	Come to Me, all you who are weary and burdened, and I will give you rest (Matt. 11:28).	Worth and Belonging
JOYFUL	Though you have not seen Him, you love Him; and even though you do not see Him now, you believe in Him and are filled with an inexpressible and glorious joy, for you are receiving the goal of your faith, the salvation of your souls (1 Pet. 1:8-9).	Worth and Belonging
JUSTIFIED	Therefore, since we have been justified through faith, we have peace with God through our Lord Jesus Christ (Rom. 5:1).	Worth and Belonging

How God Sees You	Scripture	Aspect of Identity
LIGHT OF THE WORLD	*You are the light of the world...* (Matt. 5:14).	Worth
LOVED BY GOD	*As the Father has loved Me, so have I loved you...* (John 15:9).	Worth and Belonging
MAJESTIC	*As for the saints who are in the earth, They are the majestic ones in whom is all my delight.* (Ps. 16:3 NASB)	Worth and Belonging
MEMBER OF THE BODY	*So in Christ we who are many form one body, and each member belongs to all the others* (Rom. 12:5). *Now you are the body of Christ, and each one of you is a part of it* (1 Cor. 12:27).	Belonging
MIGHTY	*His children will be mighty in the land; the generation of the upright will be blessed* (Ps. 112:2).	Belonging
NEVER ABANDONED	*Keep your lives free from the love of money and be content with what you have, because God has said, "Never will I leave you; never will I forsake you"* (Heb. 13:5).	Worth and Belonging

How God Sees You	Scripture	Aspect of Identity
NEVER ALONE	*..And surely I am with you always, to the very end of the age* (Matt. 28:20).	Worth and Belonging
NEW	*Therefore, if anyone is in Christ, he is a new creation; the old has gone, the new has come* (2 Cor. 5:17).	Worth and Belonging
OVERCOMER	*For everyone born of God overcomes the world. This is the victory that has overcome the world, even our faith* (1 John 5:4).	Worth and Belonging
PERFECT	*By one sacrifice He has made perfect forever those who are being made holy* (Heb. 10:14).	Worth and Belonging
PRECIOUS	*Since you are precious and honored in my sight* (Isa. 43:4).	Worth and Belonging
PURE	*But if we walk in the light, as He is in the light, we have fellowship with one another, and the blood of Jesus, His Son, purifies us from all sin* (1 John 1:7)	Worth and Belonging

How God Sees You	Scripture	Aspect of Identity
QUALIFIED	*Giving thanks to the Father, who has qualified you to share in the inheritance of the saints in the kingdom of light (Col. 1:12).*	Worth and Belonging
RECONCILED AND REDEEMED	*Christ redeemed us from the curse of the law by becoming a curse for us, for it is written: "Cursed is everyone who is hung on a tree" (Gal. 3:13).*	Worth and Belonging
REMEMBERED	*Can a mother forget the baby at her breast and have no compassion on the child she has borne? Though she may forget, I will not forget you! See, I have engraved you on the palms of My hands; your walls are ever before Me (Isa. 49:15-16).*	Worth and Belonging
RESCUED	*For He has rescued us from the dominion of darkness and brought us into the kingdom of the Son He loves, in whom we have redemption, the forgiveness of sins (Col. 1:13-14).*	Worth and Belonging

How God Sees You	Scripture	Aspect of Identity
RIGHTEOUS	*Put on the new self, created to be like God in true righteousness and holiness* (Eph. 4:24).	Worth and Belonging
ROYAL	*But you are a chosen people, a royal priest-hood, a holy nation, a people belonging to God, that you may declare the praises of him who called you out of darkness into His wonderful light* (1 Pet. 2:9).	Worth and Belonging
SAINT	*To the church of God in Corinth, to those sancti-fied in Christ Jesus and called to be holy* [KJV: saints]... (1 Cor. 1:2).	Worth and Belonging
SALT	*You are the salt of the earth* (Matt. 5:13)	Worth
SAVED	*Blessed are you, O Israel! Who is like you, a people saved by the Lord?* (Deut. 33:29a)	Worth and Belonging

How God Sees You	Scripture	Aspect of Identity
SERVANT OF THE LORD	*Obey them not only to win their favor when their eye is on you, but like slaves of Christ, doing the will of God from your heart. Serve wholeheartedly, as if you were serving the Lord, not men* (Eph. 6:6-7). *O Lord, truly I am Your servant; I am Your servant, the son of Your maidservant; You have freed me from my chains* (Ps. 116:16).	Worth and Belonging
SHEPHERDED	*He tends His flock like a shepherd: He gathers the lambs in His arms and carries them close to His heart; He gently leads those that have young* (Isa. 40:11). *The Lord is my shepherd, I shall not be in want. He makes me lie down in green pastures, He leads me beside quiet waters* (Ps. 23:1-2).	Worth and Belonging

How God Sees You	Scripture	Aspect of Identity
SISTER/BROTHER/ MOTHER	For whoever does the will of My Father in heaven is My brother and sister and mother (Matt. 12:50).	Belonging
SLAVE OF RIGHTEOUSNESS	You have been set free from sin and have become slaves to righteousness (Rom. 6:18).	Worth and Belonging
SOUND OF MIND	For God did not give us a spirit of timidity, but a spirit of power, of love and of self-discipline [KJV: sound mind] (2 Tim. 1:7).	Belonging
SPECIAL	But you are a chosen people, a royal priest-hood, a holy nation, (TNIV: His own special people) a people belong-ing to God, that you may declare the praises of him who called you out of darkness into his wonderful light (1 Pet. 2:9).	Worth and Belonging

How God Sees You	Scripture	Aspect of Identity
STRONG	He gives strength to the weary and increases the power of the weak (Isa. 40:29). "Do not be afraid, O man highly esteemed," he said. "Peace! Be strong now; be strong." When he spoke to me, I was strengthened and said, "Speak, my lord, since you have given me strength" (Dan. 10:19).	Worth and Belonging
STUDENT	For everything that was written in the past was written to teach us, so that through endurance and the encouragement of the Scriptures we might have hope (Rom. 15:4).	Worth and Belonging
TREASURE	For you are a people holy to the Lord your God. The Lord your God has chosen you out of all the peoples on the face of the earth to be His people, His treasured possession (Deut. 7:6).	Worth and Belonging

How God Sees You	Scripture	Aspect of Identity
UNASHAMED	*Do your best to present yourself to God as one approved, a workman who does not need to be ashamed and who correctly handles the word of truth* (2 Tim. 2:15).	Worth
UNBURDENED	*Come to me, all you who are weary and burdened, and I will give you rest* (Matt. 11:28)	Worth
UNDERSTOOD	*For we do not have a high priest who is unable to sympathize with our weaknesses, but we have one who has been tempted in every way, just as we are—yet was without sin* (Heb. 4:15).	Worth and Belonging
VALUED	*So don't be afraid; you are worth more than many sparrows* (Matt. 10:31).	Worth and Belonging
VICTORIOUS	*But thanks be to God! He gives us the victory through our Lord Jesus Christ* (1 Cor. 15:57).	Worth and Belonging

How God Sees You	Scripture	Aspect of Identity
VIRGIN	*For My virgin daughter—My people* (Jer. 14:17b). *I am jealous for you with a godly jealousy. I promised you to one husband, to Christ, so that I might present you as a pure virgin to him.* (2 Cor. 11:2B)	Belonging
WASHED	*And that is what some of you were. But you were washed, you were sanctified, you were justified in the name of the Lord Jesus Christ and by the Spirit of our God* (1 Cor. 6:11).	Belonging
WELCOME	*Here I am! I stand at the door and knock. If anyone hears My voice and opens the door, I will come in and eat with him, and he with Me* (Rev. 3:20). *Trust in Him at all times, O people; pour out your hearts to Him, for God is our refuge. Selah* (Ps. 62:8).	Worth and Belonging

How God Sees You	Scripture	Aspect of Identity
WITHOUT BLEMISH AND WITHOUT ACCUSATION	But now he has reconciled you by Christ's physical body through death to present you holy in his sight, without blemish and free from accusation (Col 1:22).	Worth and Belonging
WITHOUT CONDEMNATION	Therefore, there is now no condemnation for those who are in Christ Jesus. (Rom. 8:1)	Worth and Belonging
WORKMAN	Do your best to present yourself to God as one approved, a workman who does not need to be ashamed and who correctly handles the word of truth (2 Tim. 2:15).	Worth and Belonging
WORTHY	All this is evidence that God's judgment is right, and as a result you will be counted worthy of the kingdom of God, for which you are suffering (2 Thes. 1:5).	Worth and Belonging

About the Author

CAROL BROWN speaks in churches and provides seminars on burden bearing. To schedule her for your event or to utilize her other resources, visit her website at:

www.fromGodsheart.com.

DESTINY IMAGE PUBLISHERS, INC.

*"Speaking to the Purposes of God for This Generation
and for the Generations to Come."*

VISIT OUR NEW SITE HOME AT
WWW.DESTINYIMAGE.COM

FREE SUBSCRIPTION TO DI NEWSLETTER

Receive free unpublished articles by top DI authors, exclusive

discounts, and free downloads from our best and newest books.

Visit www.destinyimage.com to subscribe.

Write to: Destiny Image
               P.O. Box 310
               Shippensburg, PA 17257-0310

Call: 1-800-722-6774

Email: orders@destinyimage.com

For a complete list of our titles or to place an order
online, visit www.destinyimage.com.

FIND US ON FACEBOOK OR FOLLOW US ON TWITTER.

www.facebook.com/destinyimage   facebook
www.twitter.com/destinyimage   twitter

Made in the USA
Coppell, TX
20 March 2023

14482074R00160